Home Brewing

Dedication

I would like to thank my family for allowing me to experiment with trying to brew beer. Despite not having a lot of room in our home, they gave up some space for me for this new hobby I have since become very passionate about. I'd like to also thank my friends for providing me with good company and sitting down with me to test - and often help create - the perfect beer!

Disclaimer

This book is designed to provide information on home brewing only. This information is provided and sold with the knowledge that the publisher and author do not offer any legal or other professional advice. In the case of a need for any such expertise consult with the appropriate professional. This book does not contain all information available on the subject. This book has not been created to be specific to any individual's or organizations' situation or needs. Every effort has been made to make this book as accurate as possible. However, there may be typographical and or content errors. Therefore, this book should serve only as a general guide and not as the ultimate source of subject information. This book contains information that might be dated and is intended only to educate and entertain. The author and publisher shall have no liability or responsibility to any person or entity regarding any loss or damage incurred, or alleged to have incurred, directly or indirectly, by the information contained in this book. You hereby agree to be bound by this disclaimer or you may return this book within the guarantee time period for a full refund.

Foreword

DWHAHB!
Don't Worry, Have A Homebrew!

This is the mantra of home brewers.

Because you need patience for home brewing and if you make mistakes, most can be overcome or if all else fails, start again with a new batch. The main thing is to learn from mistakes as you go. Once you learn the basics of home brewing there are many ways to add your own creativity.

The investment is low and the reward is high as you will discover when you share your first great batch of beer with friends.

DWHAHB!

Table of Contents

1. Introduction to Home Brewing 11

    A (Very Brief) History of Brewing 13

    Ale to the Chief 14

    Dry Dock Brewing Co. 15

2. Brewing Processes 19

    The Three Brewing Processes 19

        Brewing Options 21

    Basic Brewing Steps 22

    Quick Definitions 23

    Beer Color 26

        Estimating Beer Color 27

    Summary 30

3. Basic Extract Beer Brewing 33

    Home Brew Kits 33

    Basic Kit Equipment 35

    The Cons of Kits 40

    Extract Beer Brewing Steps 42

    Summary 48

4. Ingredients for Home Brewing 49

Ingredients 49
    Malt Extract 49
Grains 49
    Malted Grains 52
    Unmalted Grains 53
  Hops 54
  Yeast 57
  Water 57
  Sugar (Dextrose or Glucose) 58
5. Equipment for Home Brewing 59
    Mash Paddle 61
    Hop Bags and Grain Bags 61
    Immersion Wort Chiller 62
    Counter Flow Wort Chiller 63
  More about Brew Pots 64
    Lauter Tun 65
Brewing as Art 68
6. Cleaning, Sanitation, and Sterilization 71
  Cleaning 72
  Sanitizing 73

Home Brewing

- Sterilization 73
- Sanitizers for Beer Brewing Equipment 74
- Summary 76
- 7. Partial Mash Beer Brewing 79
- 8. All Grain Beer Brewing 83
  - Mashing 86
  - Sparging 87
    - Batch Sparging 88
    - Fly Sparging 89
    - Sparging and PH 90
  - The Boil 90
  - Cooling the Wort 91
    - Pitching the Yeast 91
    - Brewing in a Bag BIAG 93
  - Summary 94
- 9. Fermenting 99
  - Specific Gravity 99
    - Stuck Fermentation 100
    - Primary and Secondary Fermentation 101
- 10. Priming and Bottling Your Beer 103

- Beer Bottle Cappers 105
- Auto Siphon 107
- Bottling Wand 108
- Kegs 109
  - Home Brewing Equipment for Kegging 110
  - Transferring Beer to a Keg 111
  - Cornelius Kegs Used In Beer Brewing 113
- DMS 115
- Summary 116
- 11. Brewing at Home Legalities 119
  - U.S. Federal Law 119
  - State Laws 121
  - Home Brewing Laws by Country 125
- Appendix 127
  - Home Brew Clubs 127
    - Australia 127
    - New Zealand 130
    - United Kingdom 130
    - United States 131
- Glossary 132

Index 137

1. Introduction to Home Brewing

The adventure of home brewing is one of the fastest growing hobbies. There are several reasons home brewing appeals to people. An appreciation for challenge is often found among beer lovers. The sense of accomplishment when you taste your first beer and enjoy the fruits of your labor is often unparalleled.

This is a hobby you can share among friends. Inviting your friends to share your home brew is fun and rewarding. You can become the center of attention at the next party. There can be great satisfaction in being recognized as the brew master and watching as your friends as they enjoy your creation. Many home brewing hobbyists have continued to pursue brewing as a money making opportunity.

When you home brew you can customize your beer to your taste preferences. You can use a simple brewing kit with a few recipes or become more involved and expand into different types of brewing with a variety of ingredients and experiment with your own. This is a hobby that is never boring.

While there is an initial investment to get started, making your own beer can produce brew that tastes better than commercially brewed beers. Learning about brewing is thrilling and though setting up your system will require some time, the brewing process is easy to monitor. Because so little time is required to monitor the fermenting process, even the busy working person has time for this hobby. You can brew beer in your home or apartment. Fermentation can be set up in an area that is out of the way.

The barrier of entry cost for home brewing is rather low. A simple equipment kit or beer machine and some ingredients can be purchased for less than $150. The 'beer machines' that can help you learn about making beer are less expensive than the kits. These offer an introduction to brewing for you to test the waters without spending too much money. You can always upgrade to an equipment kit later. The kits have equipment that adapts for more advanced brewing as you learn.

Many beer lovers are adventure seekers who like a challenge and while brewing can be kept simple and is enjoyable there many brewing methods and techniques to master so the challenges are as many as you want to pursue. You can merely brew the same tasty batch of beer again and again or experiment with brewing. Once you learn the basic methods you will discover there are numerous ways to produce beer. Home brewing allows for experimenting if you choose and even mistakes can sometimes make better beer.

There are studies that propose that a beer or two a day can be beneficial to your health. Also, homemade beers can have less hangover effects. This is due to the facts that they contain a large measure of yeast rich in Vitamin B, the beer will be absent of any preservatives, and your beer will not be delivered through a bar draft line that can contain bacteria.

Home brewing is an enjoyable hobby that can satisfy even the most curious learner. The loads of different possibilities have become an obsession for many enthusiasts.

A (Very Brief) History of Brewing

People have been brewing beer as far back as 7000 B.C. and maybe before. Without local pubs or bars and no commercial brewing, home brewing is said to be where all brewing began. Just like many things back then, if you wanted a beer you would have to make it.

In the U.S., the first President George Washington and Thomas Jefferson were both home brewers. In the 18th century the U.S. government taxed home brewing to help commercial breweries. Early in the 19th century prohibition banned all sorts of alcohol. Although prohibition was repealed later in the 1930s, not until 1979 when President Jimmy Carter passed the Cranston Act did home beer brewing again become legal. His brother, Bill Carter introduced "Billy Beer."

Home Brewing

Home brewing is enjoying an upswing in popularity. Just thirty years ago there were less than 200 beer brewing hobby stores in the U.S. and today there are over 1000. The Home Brewers Association states there are approximately 1 million people brewing at home in the U.S. This is partly due to the easily available information, ingredients, equipment, and kits on the Internet. The cost of setting up a home brewing system has decreased and there are more supplies and ingredients to choose from than ever before.

Not long ago if you wanted to home brew all that was available were malt extract, a ceramic crock and bread yeast. Now for as little as $50, there are many kits to choose from and for about another $100 in equipment you can produce five gallons of beer at a time. There have been many improvements in the home brewing process and the home enthusiast can produce a broader variety of beers, and much better quality.

Ale to the Chief

Inspired by home brewers from across the country, President Obama bought a home brewing kit for the kitchen. After the few first drafts there were some great recipes that came from a local brew shop.

The White House looked to the brewing community for home brewing tips and the staff was surprised that the beer turned out so well since none of them had brewed beer before.

As far as anyone knows the White House Honey Brown Ale is the first alcohol brewed or distilled on the White House grounds. George Washington brewed beer and distilled whiskey at Mount Vernon and Thomas Jefferson made wine but there's no evidence that any beer has been brewed in the White House.

Since the first batch of White House Honey Brown Ale, they have added the Honey Porter and a Honey Blonde.

Like many home brewers who add secret ingredients to make their beer unique, the White House brews have honey tapped from the first ever bee-hive on the South Lawn. The honey gives the beer a rich aroma and a nice finish without sweetening. .

There is a large online community of home brewers where you can learn how to brew and about new ingredients, share recipes, and troubleshoot. You can learn new ways to brew beer and decide which way you like best.

Dry Dock Brewing Co.

[1]The SBA reports that what began as a home-brew hobby has turned into a thriving brewery business for Kevin

---

[1] http://www.sba.gov

DeLange and his wife Michelle. Kevin is the President of Dry Dock Brewing Co, an Aurora base craft brewery that began in 2005. Dry Dock Brewing began winning awards for its beer as early as 2006, winning the World Beer Cup Gold H.M.S Victory ESB in the Special or Best Bitter category. Since then, Dry Dock has won 3 additional World Beer Cup awards and 11 Great American Beer Festival medals including Small Brewing Company of the Year in 2009.

Kevin and Michelle began their relationship with the U.S. Small Business Administration by utilizing SBA's 7(a) loan program. In 2009 and again in 2011 they used the 7(a) loan program to finance tenant improvements and to purchase an additional bottling machine, fermenters and kegs. They recently were approved for an SBA 504 loan to finance a 30,000 square foot building in Aurora Colorado. The new facility will house a 4-vessel, 40 barrel brew-house that will eventually be capable of producing more than 60,000 barrels of beer per year (one barrel is 31 U.S. gallons). Their goal is to brew 12,000 barrels in the first year. In addition to utilizing SBA's loan guaranty programs, Kevin is a participant in the 2012 SBA Emerging 200 Initiative – a 7-month curriculum that enables participants to engage in focused development and expansion strategies for their business.

Home Brewing

Since opening, Dry Dock Brewing has never been able to keep up with the demand for their award-winning beer. Kevin and Michelle's approach to growth has been incremental and slow – all part of their plan to grow from a small brewery to a medium-sized brewery. Their production has grown from 300 barrels in 2006 to 3,200 barrels projected for 2012. On a typical Friday night, the brewery will pour 15 barrels or 4,200 glasses of beer. Pretty impressive for a guy from Iowa whose business started as a hobby!

2. Brewing Processes

The Three Brewing Processes

Although the beer brewing processes are basically the same there are numerous diverse techniques to produce the brew. There are certain parameters to follow in home brewing to stay safe and get the best results though there is no single right way for home brewing. Once you learn about the processes, you will discover that part of the challenge of home brewing is that beyond the fundamental principles there are many ways to experiment.

There are three basic methods of home brewing:

1. Extract brewing
2. Partial mash brewing
3. All grain brewing

The definitions closely follow the titles making the three methods easy to remember.

Extract Brewing utilizes malt extract and no grains. This method is usually recommended for beginners. This is a straightforward, stripped down process that can teach you the basics of brewing. Even this method will allow for adjustments and some experimenting.

Extract brewing is the easiest and all grain brewing the most difficult. Partial mash and all grain brewing both require more steps and ingredients though they give you more power over your final product. As you gain experience brewing, you can try each method and experiment with countless variations of brewing.

Partial Mash Brewing is a combination of malt extract and grains. With partial mash brewing you add grains to your boil as well as some malt extract. You can first steep the grains, and that process is similar to making tea. You add the grains to your boil directly or in a grain bag.

This will pull out flavors and colors from the grains for your completed beer. When steeping is complete you mash the grains. This is a partial mash. Partial mashing referred to sometimes as mini mashing, enables you to bring in base malt from grains, and *mashing is all grain brewing.* A full mash is "All Grain Brewing."

All Grain Brewing uses no extract and all grain, is more complex than extract brewing, and takes longer. You will need to be exact with amounts and measurements and maintain an accurate temperature. You can produce more types of beer and have more options to experiment with all grain brewing. Again, mashing is all grain brewing.

Brewing Options

You can produce flavorful beers to your liking with the more complex methods. You can stay with the method of extract brewing or try the more difficult methods.

The majority of brewing enthusiasts begin by brewing with a kit, and that is extract brewing. If you want more control over your final product the next step is to add steeped specialty grains to the brew. Steeping grains will help you get flavors that you cannot get from extract alone.

The next level is to partial mash. This is where you substitute some of the malt extract with grain.

Home Brewing

All grain brewing is the most advanced process where brew is made completely from grains and no malt extract.

Basic Brewing Steps

1. Obtaining Equipment and Ingredients
2. Sanitation
3. Making the Wort
4. Heating the Wort
5. Adding the hops
6. Cooling or Chilling the Wort
7. Fermenting
8. Priming and Bottling
9. Storing / Aging / Bottle Conditioning

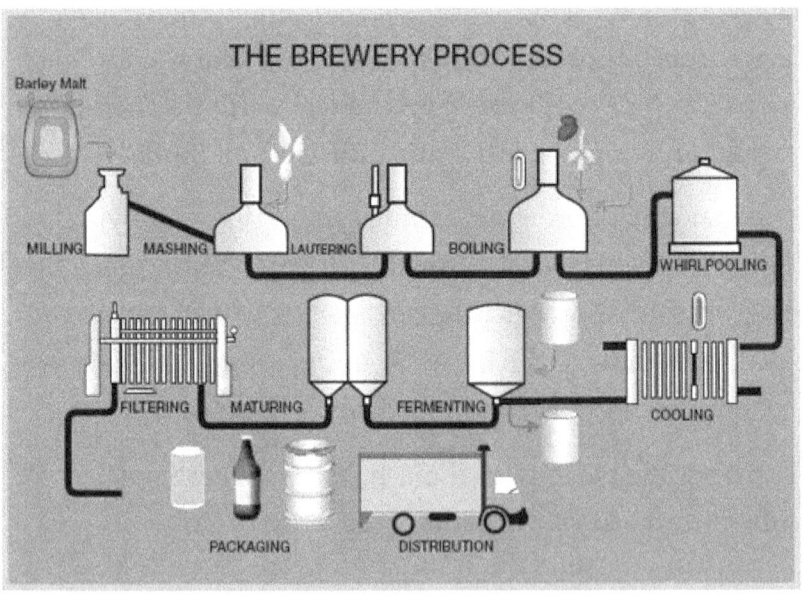

Image Source: http://www.monarch-beverage.com

Quick Definitions

Bottle-conditioning: Bottle conditioning is when the beer is given extra time for fermenting in the bottle. Sometimes carbonation, yeast or sugars are added.

Mashing: The home brewing term for steeping malt and other grains in hot water to extract the starches from the grain and convert them to sugar.

Wort (pronounced "Wert"): The beer liquid (typically the malted grains and water which is sugar rich) or raw beer before fermenting with yeast. The wort is boiled with hops before cooling and adding yeast to start fermentation.

Enzymes: Proteins that cause chemical reactions and accelerate the fermentation process. The chief source of enzymes in the brewing procedure is malt barley.

Fermentation: The process of fermentable sugars in the wort being consumed by the yeast subsequently producing alcohol and carbon dioxide.

Top-Fermenting Yeast: Used to produce Ales or beer that has a fruit taste and can stand higher alcohol concentrations.

Bottom-Fermenting Yeast: For a crisp clean taste such as in Lagers.

Racking: This is the transferring of wort or beer from the brew pot to the fermenter whether for primary or secondary fermentation.

Siphon: The tube and process used to transfer wort from fermentation to the bottling bucket.

Trub: This is proteins from the grains used in brewing and left behind at the bottom of the fermenter after the wort has been removed.

Sparging: Upon the completion of steeping grains and filtering them out of the wort, this is the heating of additional water to rinse the grains in a colander to remove as much sugar and flavor from the grains as possible.

Partial/Full boil: A partial boil is 2 or 3 gallons and full boil is 5 gallons. Partial boils are used in extract home brewing and later top off water is added to make 5 gallons. All grain home brewing requires full boils.

Primary fermentation: When wort becomes beer through the conversion of sugars into alcohol and carbon dioxide. Yeast causes this conversion under the right conditions.

Secondary fermentation: Conditioning and clearing the beer not additional fermentation.

Specific Gravity (SG): This is a key measurement in brewing that tells you when fermentation is finished and how efficient the process was or what amount of the obtainable sugar was converted to alcohol. A hydrometer is used to measure specific gravity.

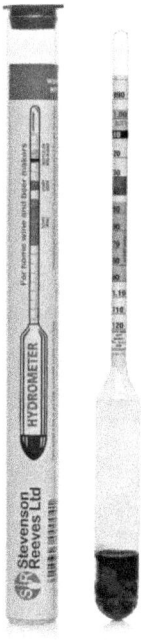

Hydrometer

Image Source: http://www.wilko.com

Beer Color

Beers come in an infinite display of colors. Dark beers can be deep black and Bavarian wheat light amber. Beer color is measured by a system created back in 1883 by J.W. Lovibond. This is called the Lovibond color, although now light spectrophotometer is also used to determine color and measured with the Standard Reference Method (SRM.) The SRM color is similar the Lovibond scale. There is also the

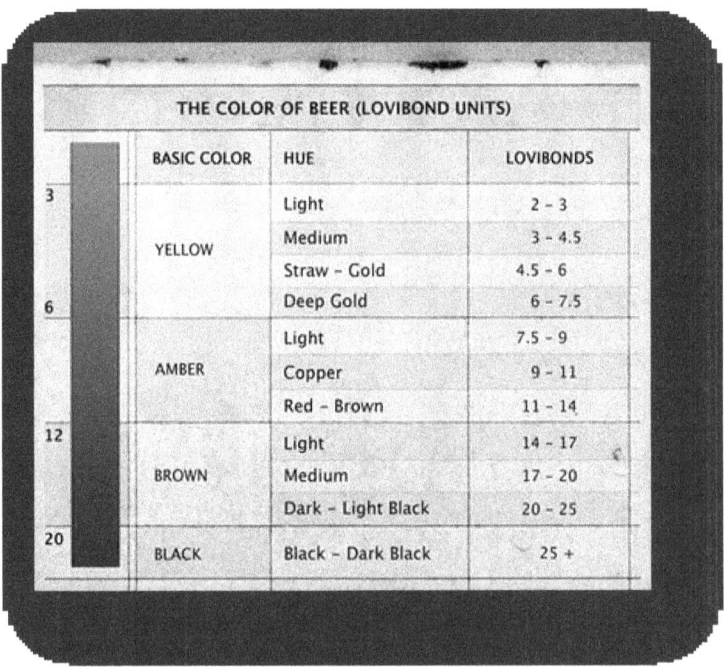

European Brewing Convention (EBC) standard of measure.

Lovibond Chart

Image Source: http://www.orionhomebrewing.com

Home Brewing

Because most home brewers do not have a spectrophotometer a beer reference color card, such as the SRM chart or Davidson guide, can help you make a visual comparison of your brew.

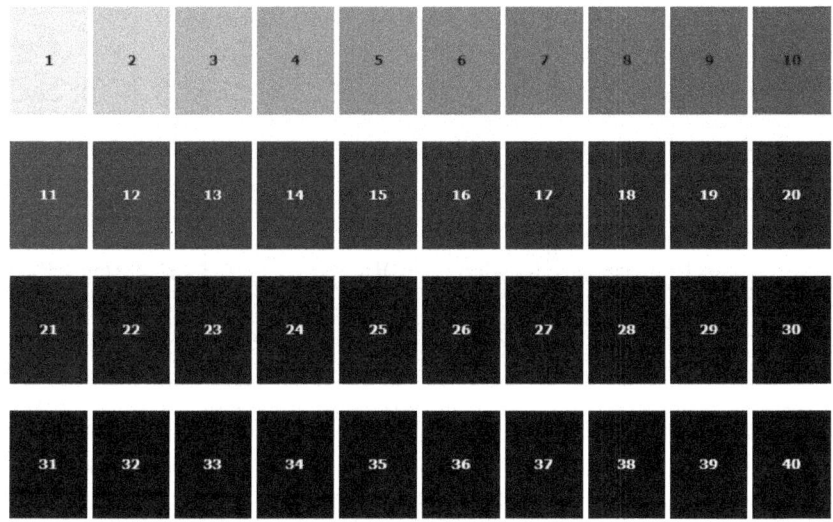

SRM Beer Color Chart
Image Source: www.homebrewtalk.com

Estimating Beer Color

There are countless variations of red, brown, gold, copper, orange, yellow, amber and straw. While beer color is not an exact science and there are limitations you can estimate the color of your brew.

There are several formulas for estimating beer color. The first involves calculating the Malt Color Units (MCUs) of your recipe.

$$\text{MCU} = (\text{Weight of grain in lbs}) \times (\text{Color of grain in degrees lovibond}) / (\text{volume in gallons})$$

If you are using several grains, calculate the MCU for each one and then total the results. MCU presents a fairly good estimate of the SRM color for light beers.

For darker beers the Morey equation gives better results.

$$\text{SRM color} = 1.4922 * (\text{MCU}^{0.6859})$$

Extract brewers need to be aware that

The liquid extracts for extract brewing often get darker with age. Extracts also darken in a carmelization process during boiling.

Again most home brewers begin with a kit and extract brewing. With a kit you pour the malt extract into the wort. The extract can be in liquid or dry form.

Just because extract brewing is the process most beginners use does not mean your beer can only be mediocre. Award winning beers have been produced through extract brewing.

A kit is a great way to learn about home brewing through experience. There are some limitations to kit brewing although with a few modifications you can produce some great beer.

Extract brewing will teach you the fundamentals of home brewing. As you gain experience with extract brewing under you might want to move up to partial mash brewing. You can even skip to all grain brewing if you prefer. There are so many variations of ingredients and styles you will have endless options. The more advanced brewing processes involve making your own wort by boiling hops and barley and then chilling the wort and pitching yeast. Other than that the processes are much the same as kit brewing.

While many hobbyists see starting with extract brewing and then moving to partial mash, and then all grain as the order of things, your preferences, budget, space available, and results can all dictate the order and processes you choose. You can stick with extract brewing, skip a process, or tweak a process to your liking. You can stay with kit brewing or build a brewing system with more steps.

Summary

There are **three basic methods** types of home brewing:

1. Extract brewing
2. Partial mash brewing
3. All grain brewing

Extract Brewing utilizes malt extract and no grains and is recommended for beginners. Most home brewers begin with a kit and extract brewing. With a kit you pour the malt extract into the wort. The extract can be in liquid or dry form. Extract brewing will teach you the fundamentals of home brewing.

Partial Mash Brewing is a combination of malt extract and grains. When steeping is complete you mash the grains. This is a partial mash. A full mash is "All Grain Brewing."

All Grain Brewing uses no extract and all grain, is more complex than extract brewing, and takes longer.

The more advanced brewing processes involve making your own wort by boiling hops and barley and then chilling the wort and pitching yeast. Other than that the processes are much the same as kit brewing.

Home Brewing

Basic Brewing Steps

1. Obtaining Equipment and Ingredients
2. Sanitation
3. Making the Wort
4. Heating the Wort
5. Adding the hops
6. Cooling or Chilling the Wort
7. Fermenting
8. Priming and Bottling
9. Storing / Aging / Bottle Conditioning

Specific Gravity is a key measurement in brewing that tells you when fermentation is finished and how efficient the process was and is measured using a hydrometer.

3. Basic Extract Beer Brewing

Home Brew Kits

There are many possibilities for beer brewing and a diverse array of equipment options. Base your equipment decisions on your budget, experience, the space you have available for your brewery. You can buy equipment piece by piece, use certain house hold items, purchase a kit, make some of the equipment, or a combination of these.

For beginners a kit (or sometime referred to as an ingredient kit) is recommended as they are less expensive, convenient, and give you an opportunity to familiarize yourself with the process and decide if you like home brewing. Home brew kits have grown in popularity as the process is being perfected. Kits usually include fairly foolproof instructions and ingredients. There are a lot of diverse home brewing kits available and each one is designed for a different customer type. Some cater to the beginner; others are for the more casual home brewer, and still others are designed for advanced hobbyists.

Kits include a beer can or premade wort. This saves you a great deal of time. You mix the premade wort with sugar or a mixture of malts and add water as instructed. Then the yeast is pitched and fermentation commences. After the

Home Brewing

fermentation period you bottle your beer and let it age. The longer beer ages the more taste and consistency develops.

Images Source: http://ziazu.com
Beer Kit

Home Brewing

Basic Kit Equipment

A list of basic equipment includes:

Air Lock: Each carboy will need an airlock and a rubber stopper that fits the opening.

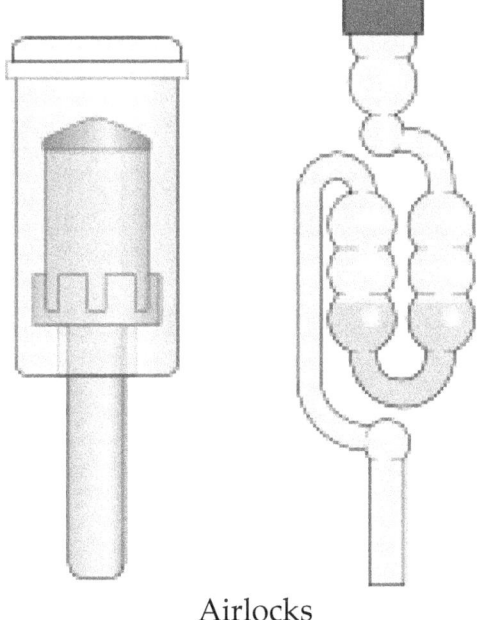

Airlocks

Bottle Brushes: Several sizes.

Bottles, Caps, and Bottle Capper

Bottle Filler: Rigid plastic tube with a tip spring loaded valve for filling the bottles.

Brew Pot and Lid: A five gallon stainless steel pot and lid made of stainless steel, aluminum or enamel coated aluminum. Plain steel should be avoided because the steel can influence the flavor of the beer. The pot capacity must be at least three gallons and preferably five gallons.

Image Source: www.porterhousebrewshop.com

Brew Pot

Home Brewing

Carboy: This is a large glass or stainless steel bottle also known as a demijohn used in fermentation. Beer is transferred or siphoned from the carboy into bottles for aging, priming, or conditioning. (The transferring is referred to as racking.) The carboy is typically fitted with a rubber stopper and fermentation lock to keep bacteria and oxygen out of the fermentation process.

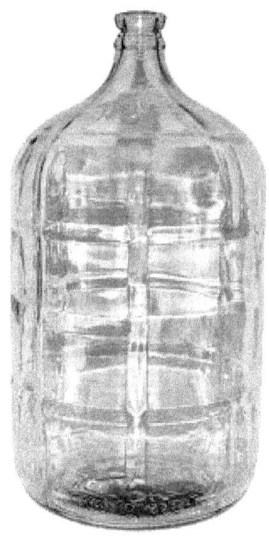

Image Source: www.homebrewers.com

Carboy

Fermentation Bucket: - This should be a "food grade" bucket of five to six and a half gallons.

5 Gallon Bucket

Stainless Steel Spoon: A two foot long stainless steel spoon.

Siphon Tube: Clear plastic tubing.

Home Brewing

Racking Cane: Rigid plastic or stainless steel tube with sediment stand-off used to siphon without transferring the trub.

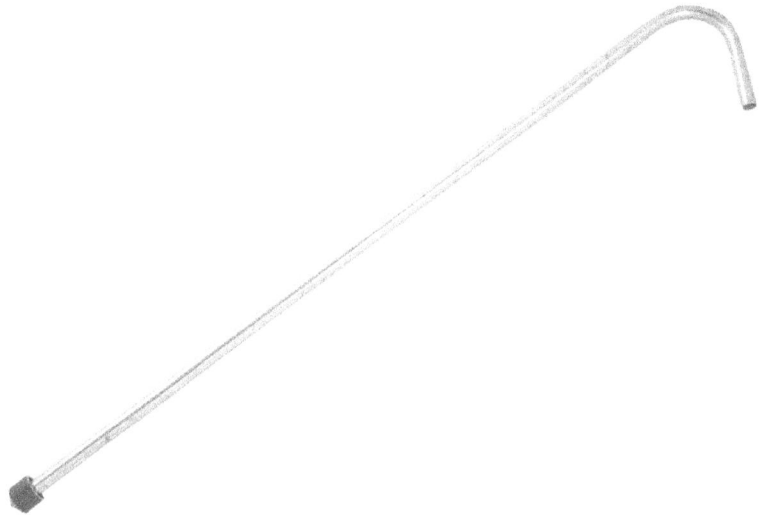

Image Source: www.homebrewers.com

Racking Cane

Sanitizing Solution: Chemical sanitizers must be used to eliminate most of the bacteria on the equipment.

All the equipment will generally be a cost of $125 to $200. One difference is the cost of a glass carboy versus a stainless steel one. A stainless steel carboy is lighter and less prone to breaking.

Beginners should start with beer kits that consist of individual components to learn the basics of brewing. These kits usually contain the basics without needing to spend a fortune. When you have brewed a few batches and understand the process you can decide if you are satisfied with your kit or upgrade or move up a level in the beer brewing process.

Your first upgrade can be ingredients. You still use the equipment in your kit but can experiment with ingredients to experience different results.

You might also want to purchase an additional fermenter to make more beer. Plastic buckets designed for fermenting are standard with many brewing kit though you can upgrade these to glass or stainless steel carboys. However there is no problem fermenting in plastic buckets.

The Cons of Kits

There are several drawbacks to kits that are easy to overcome. One thing is the ingredients are not always the best yet you can buy fresh yeast and hops to your boil for a better tasting beer. As you learn the process your beer will improve.

Because the kits usually include pre-hopped malt extract the flavor of your beer might not be the greatest. Fresh hops are often a dramatic improvement. You just add the fresh hops to your boil and remove or filter them out previous to fermentation.

Also, your kit instructions might leave a bit to be desired. They can be vague, missing details, and even lacking the best advice. For example, often these instructions will state that a week is long enough for fermenting. The longer your beer ferments the better and four to eight weeks is usually needed. Kits that recommend bottling within 5-10 days are probably of poor quality.

Even with these drawbacks most brew kits are great for beginners to learn how to make beer. When you have the basics down you can experiment and see how even small changes can influence your results.

Award winning beers have been produced from extract brewing and kits. A few brewing snobs might knock the kits, but many of them started with one.

Extract Beer Brewing Steps

Keep a brewing notebook and take notes of every brew. Then on your future brews you can make changes or corrections from your notes.

1. Clean and sanitize all equipment.

Clean then sanitize all your equipment and keep a spray bottle of sanitizer around to sanitize again as needed.

2. Prepare the water.

Boil water for 15 minutes to eliminate all chlorine first.

3. Prepare the ingredients

When using an ingredient kit this will be but a small number of ingredients. Advanced kits will often be comprised of specialty grains and mesh bags and sometimes you will need to crush the grains first before steeping. A rolling pin works well for crushing.

4. Boil the water and add ingredients.

1. Bring the water to a boil and then remove from the heat source.
2. Add the malt extract stirring meticulously to prevent the extract from sinking to the bottom where it can get scorched.
3. Replace the pot on the heat for a period as specified by your instructions. Do not let the pot boil over.

4. Add hops: If using bitter hops add them right away and if using flavoring hops add them near the end.

5. Cool your Wort

1. Remove the heat and quickly cool to less than 80 degrees F. You can even place the pot in ice or purchase an immersion chiller.
2. When the wort has reached the right temperature, transfer it to the fermenter.

Be careful when moving your wort. While splashing or sloshing during the transfer will not harm your brew, this can introduce bacteria from the air at any other time. Oxygen will help the yeast in this phase but any other time air is the enemy when brewing.

When extract brewing you will probably only be partial boiling. This means rather than brewing five gallons of wort you will top off with water to equal a total of five gallons batch. Topping off the water also eliminates any need to aerate your wort for the yeast.

6. Add yeast.

Your instructions will tell you how much yeast to add and if you have dry yeast you must rehydrate it in warm water previous to pitching.

7. Take a Hydrometer Reading

Now take a hydrometer reading to establish your Original Gravity (OG). Then you will have a comparison point later after fermentation has completed.

Home Brewing

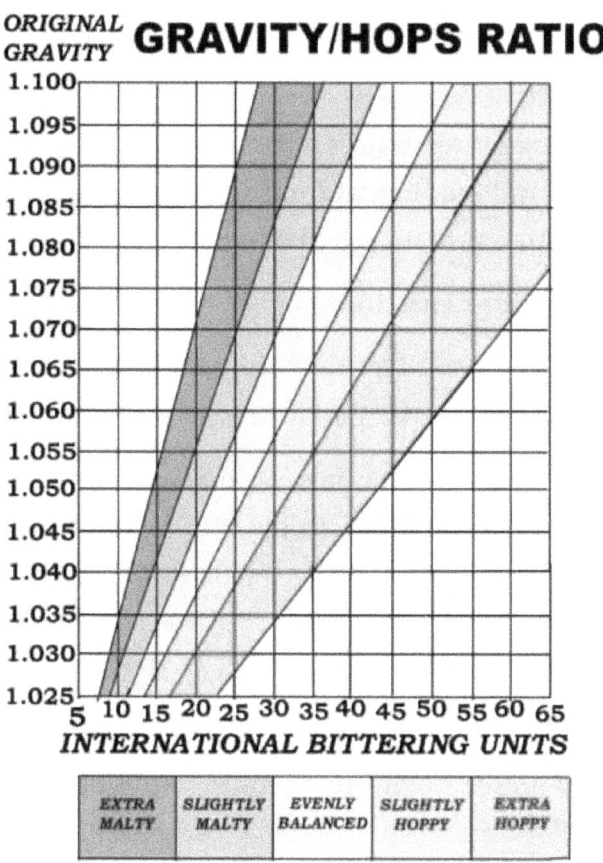

Image Source: www.homebrewtalk.com

8. Fermentation

Your kit instructions should advise temperature and final gravity. Now you seal the fermenter and insert the airlock. Keep your soon to be beer at the recommended temperature throughout fermentation which should be about ten days, however three or four weeks will produce better beer.

Take hydrometer readings on consecutive days. When you get the identical reading within five points of your final gravity goal fermentation will be complete.

9. Secondary fermentation

The purpose of secondary fermentation is to clarify and condition. This is not needed for many kinds of beers.

Some brewers use a secondary fermenter and others leave their brew in the primary fermenter.

10. Bottle your Beer

When fermentation is complete you can package your beer.

1. Sanitizing

Bottles and bottling equipment must be sanitized. This includes all tubing, wands, siphon, caps, and so on.

2. Sugar Additive

Some kits suggest adding sugar or a sugar mix.

- Boil a quart of water, add the sugar, and let the sugar dissolve.
- When the mix cools to 70 degrees put that in the bottling bucket.
- Carefully rack your beer into the bottling bucket.

3. Siphoning

Home Brewing

An automatic siphon is an advantage in over mouth siphoning as using your mouth introduces bacteria into your brew.

4. Priming/Aging

When your beer is bottled and capped allow a few weeks for your beer to prime and carbonate.

Summary

Home Brew Kits

For beginners a kit (or sometime referred to as an ingredient kit) is recommended as they are less expensive, convenient, and give you an opportunity to familiarize yourself with the process and decide if you like home brewing. There are many possibilities for beer brewing and a diverse array of equipment options

When you have brewed a few batches and understand the process you can decide if you are satisfied with your kit or upgrade or move up a level in the beer brewing process. Your first upgrade can be ingredients. There are several drawbacks to kits but they are easy to overcome.

Extract Beer Brewing Steps

1. Sanitize all equipment.
2. Prepare the water.
3. Prepare the ingredients
4. Boil the water and add ingredients.
5. Cool your Wort
6. Add yeast.
7. Take a Hydrometer Reading
8. Fermentation
9. Secondary fermentation
10. Bottle your Beer

4. Ingredients for Home Brewing

While home brewing with a brew kit provides most of what you need, if you want to build your own system or advance to the other brewing processes (partial mash or all grain brewing) there are ingredients and equipment to buy.

Ingredients

Malt Extract

Malting is the process of converting barley or other cereal grains into malt, for use in brewing. Malt Extract is created by the forced germination of barley grain. This stimulates the enzymes used for brewing beer. You can buy pre-made malt extract at a brewing store or online retailer. There are scores of different flavors and varieties.

Grains

When you are extract brewing your grains are prepared. If you choose partial mash or all grain brewing, you will be using grains.

Brewing grains are second only to water in beer ingredients. The sugars required for yeast fermentation come from grains. They give beer color, flavor, texture, and foam.

Malted barley is the most common brewing grain and corn wheat, oats, rice, and rye are also used. Malt is cereal grain that has been through the malting process. The malting process is the kilning and managed germination of grain. Kilning is the heating of grain in an oven.

Malting is a process that causes grains to convert starch to sugar during brewing. Malted grain is also used for making whiskey, malted milk shakes, and malt vinegar.

The Malting Process is done in three steps called steeping and germination, drying, and kilning.

Steeping and Germination: The grains are steeped (placed in hot water) for 38 to 46 hours. They will double in weight from water absorption.

After steeping they are drained and placed in a germination area with a controlled environment for four days. Germination is a part of the plant's natural growth cycle. Enzymes in the grains are activated and measured by a term called modification. Highly modified malt has had a major amount of enzyme development and starch conversion.

Drying: Now the malt is put into a kiln (oven) and dried for about 24 to 36 hours with heat at 121 to 158 degrees F. Certain malts such as base malts are now complete.

Kilning: Some grains are heated at higher temperatures for longer times to give them distinctive colors and flavors. The amount of time in the kiln and the temperature result in lighter or darker malts. Roasted malts are referred to as specialty grains.

Caramelization is a chemical reaction during kilning when the sugar in the grain breaks down for sweet flavors.

A *maillard reaction* is a darkening of the grain caused by the amino acids and sugars interacting. These malts have more bready or toasty flavors.

There are four categories of malts determined by the period of time and temperature in the kiln and the moisture level during kilning. They are:

- base malts
- crystal or caramel malts
- toasted malts
- roasted malts

Base Malts: Low temperature kilning of base malts lets them retain the most potential sugar. Because of this base malts are typically 85% of brew recipes. Base malts are always made from barley or wheat. Pilsner, pale ale, Munich, and Vienna are common base malts.

Caramel or Crystal Malts: Caramel is the American version of malt and Crystal is the English name for the same malt. Caramel malts are roasted after germination rather than dried. This causes enzymes that convert starches into sugars in the grain to be activated. Lighter caramel malts have honey and caramel flavors and the darker caramel malts have rich toffee and raisin flavors. Beers produced from caramel malts include American Amber Ales, English Bitters, and Scottish ales.

Toasted Malts: Toasted malts are heated to higher temperatures over 300 degrees F for darker colors and a toast or nut taste. Some toasted malts include aromatic, amber, and brown malt and use for brown ales and bocks.

Roasted Malts: These are the darkest malts and have the richest flavors. They are less common and used in Porters and Stouts.

Malted Grains

Malted Barley: Barley is the most preferred grain for brewing. Barley is a grass and has been cultivated for thousands of years.

Wheat: Wheat is the second most popular malted grain and has also been cultivated for many centuries. There is more protein in wheat than barley and so using wheat results in rich full and sometimes cloudy beers.

Oats & Rye: Rye is becoming more popular in craft beers and adds a unique spicy taste to beer. Malted oats are rarely used for beer. Oats and rye each require the use of malted barley for suitable starch conversion.

Unmalted Grains

Unmalted grains are referred to as adjuncts. These grains lighten color, add certain flavors, and are used for producing beer that is gluten free. Unmalted or adjunct grains include barley, corn, rice, rye, oats, and wheat.

Corn: Corn is used in producing American lagers and English Bitters. Corn can lighten color without affecting flavor.

Rice: This adjunct grain can lighten color and texture or body. Rice is found in some lagers and used by craft brewers.

Wheat: Wheat can also be used unmalted to increase the effects of the wheat.

Barley: Unmalted barley can augment body and help maintain the head.

Rye: Unmalted rye is also utilized for augmenting body, to help maintain the head, and achieve more of the characters of the rye.

Oats: Oats provide unique flavor and improve body and head retention.

Hops

Hops come from the hop flower. Hops are the female flowers of the hop plant. They are used to give beer bitterness, aroma, and other flavoring described as outdoors, grassy, floral, citrus, spicy, lemon, grapefruit, and earthy. They also work as a preservative.

The hop cones have resins that flavor beer and create foam. Hops also have an antibacterial effect that allows the activity of brewer's yeast over undesirable microorganisms.

The hop plant grows on twine or string in a hop field, hop garden, or hop yard. There are an assortment of hops grown for different beers and brewing processes.

[2]Van Burnette's hop yard in Buncombe Co

Hops are grown around the world and are not hard to cultivate. Some home brewers grow their own hops for brewing.

The two main hop types are; bittering and aroma. These come from their oils and resins. Oils contribute aroma and flavor, and resins are responsible for bitterness. The oils boil off sooner and the resins take a longer time.

The bittering hops have high concentrations of alpha acids. Resins take longer to boil off the wort so the bittering hops

---

[2] http://ncalternativecropsandorganics.blogspot.com/2010/10/new-nc-hops-project-website-check-it.html

are added sooner to the wort to boil longer, often for an hour to an hour and a half. The amount of bitterness is measured in IBUs (International Bitterness Units.) IBUs are a measurement amount of alpha acid.

Aroma hops are added to the wort during the final half hour of the boil. This keeps them from boiling off the entire aroma. Sometimes aroma hops are added after the wort has cooled and during fermentation. This is referred to as "dry hopping."

Although there are well over 200 components of the hop oils, the three chief elements of the essential oil of hops include are myrcene, humulene, and caryophyllene. The makeup of hop essential oils can fluctuate a great deal between varieties and harvests of the same variety. There are also dual hops that contain high concentrations of alpha acids and aromatic elements that can be put in the wort any time during the boil.

Home brewing hops can be found as whole, dried hops, (preferred for dry hopping), hops pellets, which have a longer shelf life, and hop plugs.

Noble Hops

Noble hops are a variety of hops that have modest bitterness yet are rich in aroma. There are four hops classified as the Noble Hops: Hallertau, Tettnanger, Spalt and Saaz. They have large amounts of oil, and small amounts of acids making them aromatic. Noble hops are used for European lager beers for instance Pilsener, Dunkel, or Oktoberfest.

Yeast

Yeast is a fungus, a living organism with many variations from around the world. This fungus helps convert sugar in the malt extract into alcohol and carbon dioxide. Yeast is a used as an ingredient in numerous baking and brewing processes. Brewing yeast is indispensable in the wort fermentation to chemically alter the makeup of the brew and create an alcohol content.

Brewing yeast has two primary features; the top fermenting yeast and the bottom fermenting yeast. Yeast does not always perform at levels but works through the entire wort mixture. Top fermenting yeast cooks at higher temperatures, typically 60 or 75 degrees F. This contributes to a sweet taste such as ale beers have and results in higher alcohol content. Yeast fermenting at the bottom at a lower temperature sometimes produces a crisp flavor such as with a lager style beer.

Water

Filtered water or boiled tap water.

Sugar (Dextrose or Glucose)

Sugar carbonates beer. Sugar or a mixture of sugar and water boiled and then cooled is added to the beer at the time of bottling.

5. Equipment for Home Brewing

While some of the equipment has been covered for the kits and extract brewing, here is a quick equipment list for the other processes:

Brewpot: Where the malt extract, water and hops are mixed and boiled. This is usually a 5 gallon or larger stainless steel pot.

Fermenter: A fermenter is basically any type of vessel that can be used to contain the beer as it is being fermented. A sturdy plastic bucket, pail or glass carboy is the most widespread types of fermenters.

Funnel and Strainer: For transferring the brew from the pot to the fermenter.

Siphon Hose: This is for bottling when you transfer beer from the fermenter. An auto-siphon is best to avoid contamination.

Airlock: Prevents outside air from getting inside the fermenter, and allows the carbon dioxide produced by fermentation to escape.

Thermometer: You need to take the temperature of your brew at different times while brewing. There are stick-on thermometers that enable temperature measurement without risking any contamination by sticking a thermometer in your brew.

Bottling Bucket: For finished beer and priming solution for bottling.

Propane Burner

A propane burner can heat wort faster than most household stoves. If you have access to an outdoor area to boil your wort, this can reduce the boil time.

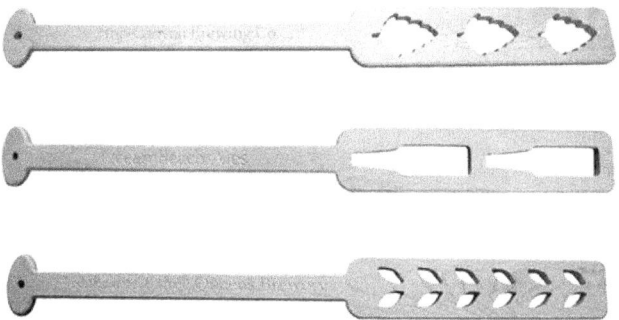

Mash Paddle

Images Source: drinks.seriouseats.com

Hop Bags and Grain Bags

Hop bags and grain steeping bags mesh bags used for steeping grains. Hop bags are made with two mesh sizes:

- fine mesh for the pellets
- medium mesh for whole hops (A medium mesh bag is also used for steeping grains.)

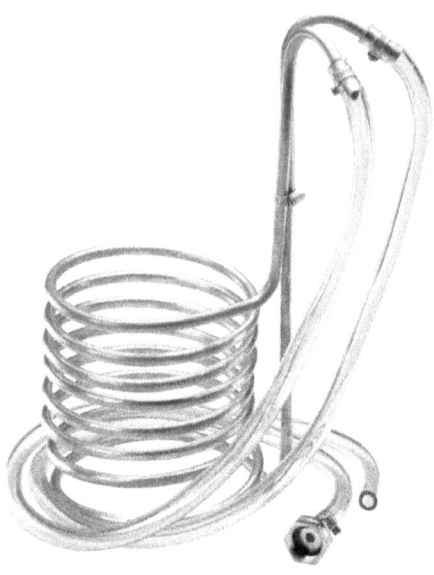

Image Source: www.mainbrew.com

Immersion Wort Chiller

Home brewers use the immersion chiller, counter-flow (CF) chiller or ice. Choosing between the immersion and counter-flow chillers is a matter of preference, however the immersion chiller is less expensive and easier to use and clean although the counter flow chiller is said to be more effective. The immersion chiller works slower than the CF chiller. Also the risk of contamination is a bit more due to the chilling happening in an open pot.

The immersion chiller is single copper tubing coil (between 25 and 50 feet long.) The coil is immersed inside the brew pot. When cold water is pumped through the copper tubing the wort is cooled.

Image Source: homebrewdownunder.com

Counter Flow Wort Chiller

The counter flow (CF) chiller is a heat exchanger. This is made of copper tubing that runs inside a rubber hose or another larger diameter copper tube. There are fittings on the ends for cool water to run in one direction in the larger tube while the hot wort runs in the opposite direction (counter flow) in the smaller tube. Running the liquids in opposite directions is more efficient. The length of the tube is usually 25 feet and as this setup is more complex it is also more expensive.

More about Brew Pots

The brew pot, or brew kettle is a chief component of your brewing system and should be made of stainless steel, aluminum or enamel coated aluminum because plain steel can negatively flavor beer. A great brew pot can last for years and make tons of beer.

If you use an aluminum pot there are a few procedures. A new aluminum pot must be seasoned once before use. The inside of the pot is oxidized by filling with water and boiling and that will change the color of the inside of the pot. The aluminum oxide coating forms a protective layer between the aluminum and anything boiled such as your wort.

Do not clean aluminum with abrasive detergents, scouring pads, steel wool or oxygen based cleaners. These cleaners and methods will remove the protective oxidation layer and can damage or scratch the pot. Scratched aluminum can also harbor bacteria.

The stainless steel or aluminum pot must be at least three gallons and bigger is better as common batch amount is five gallons so a six gallon pot will give you the extra room needed to avoid boiling over. You can also do a partial boil where you make smaller batches at a time and then add them to the fermenter.

Home Brewing

You need to also consider your heat source when choosing a brew pot size. While an outdoor propane burner is ideal, if your space is limited and you are brewing indoors in an apartment for example, you might be limited to using a stove for heat. Many stoves cannot generate the heat needed to bring a large pot to boil in a practical time period. If this is the case you can do partial boils in smaller pots.

Lauter Tun

A lauter tun is the conventional pot used in the more sophisticated all grain brewing process that separates the extracted wort. The device has a false bottom that has a screen to collect a runoff of wort. This is created when the sparge water is poured over the grains. The false bottom

holds back solids and allows liquids to pass through. The solids form a filtration medium and retain small solids permitting the mash to run out as a clear liquid.

A small lauter tun can be 15 gallons that will contain up to 35 pounds of grain. The run off tubes are evenly distributed across the bottom.

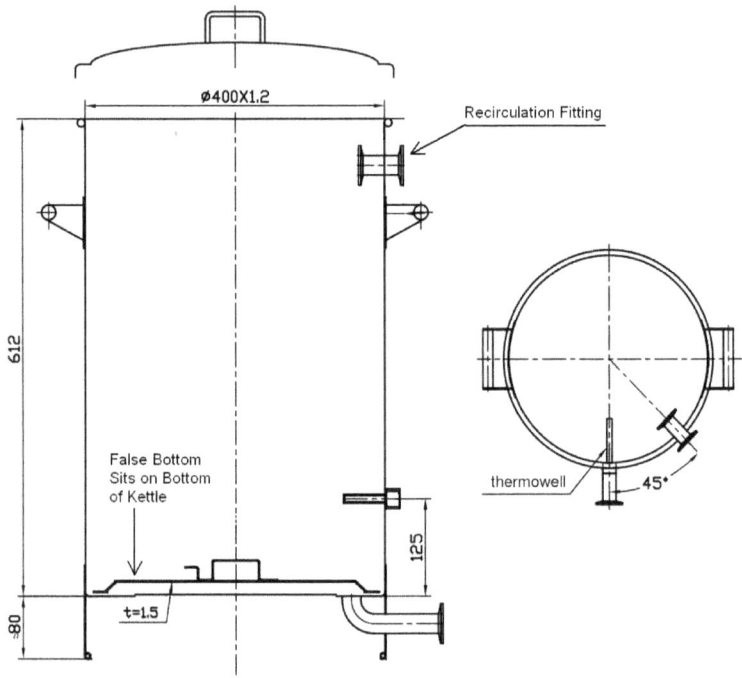

Image Source: http://conical-fermenter.com/products/mash-tuns/

Lauter Tun Diagram

Sophisticated lauter tuns have rotating rake arms with cutting blades with flaps that push grains out of the tun. Sparge water is sprayed evenly into the tun.

Some home brewers make 'home-made' lauter tuns.

Home Brewing

Image Source: http://vintage63brewing.wordpress.com/2011/11/25/more-beer-1550-tippy-brew-sculpture/

Brewing as Art

Home brewing systems are often referred to as sculptures because of their unique aesthetic designs. [3]Brewing as art sculpture is taking home brewing to new heights. These are functional home brewing systems that are challenging common perceptions of art.

This design is by Mark Zappasodi of the New Brighton Homebrew Society and Scott Van Campen. Scott is a metal sculptor by trade and their mobile sculpture is designed after the Victorian "steampunk" style tied in with Staten

---

[3] http://www.homebrewersassociation.org

Home Brewing

Island's rich 150 year brewing history. The sculpture is fabricated by hand apart from a few vital mechanisms.

The core of the project is to illustrate that crafting fine beer really is an art form that has ties to alchemy, religion, and shared experiences with others.

The Brewing as Art sculpture has served a Maritime Ale, well-hopped amber ale; a Dusseldorf Old Ale, a German ale with a large malt character similar to an English bitter; and Gingerfoot Saison.

6. Cleaning, Sanitation, and Sterilization

Clean brewing equipment makes clean beer, and clean beer always tastes better. Home brewing requires diligent sanitizing, which is not just cleaning. Proper sanitizing helps prevent bacteria and germs from contaminating and ruining your beer. Beer brewing is 75% sanitation. *Purportedly, the number one cause for poor tasting beer is poor sanitation.*

If you do not thoroughly clean your equipment before sanitizing, your equipment will have residue that harbors germs and bacteria. This makes sanitizing impossible. Proper cleaning is imperative to good sanitation. Clean and sanitized equipment is required to make great beer.

This is why certain precautions are critical such as sanitizing beer brewing equipment. Chemical sanitizers must be used in the beer brewing process to eliminate the majority of the microorganisms on the equipment beyond what simple soap and water can accomplish alone. Developing sanitation habits will help you produce good beer every time.

The yeast needs a healthy environment while fermenting. Fermentation is controlled yeast growing that healthy environment for yeast is the same healthy environment for germs and bacteria. Sanitizing equipment keeps contaminants to a minimum.

Again, clean your equipment first and then sanitize the apparatus. There is a difference between cleaning, sanitizing and sterilizing.

Cleaning

Cleaning is generally defined as a visible process of removing residue and dirt. There are many agents that will remove dirt, but do not eradicate a considerable number of microorganisms. Cleaning is needed but prior to and in addition to sanitizing.

Some cleaning products do better on some surfaces than others so after you try them you might find yourself using several different cleaners.

OxyClean is very effective and a popular preference in home brewing. OxyClean is available in grocery stores. The other discount brand oxygen based cleaners work just as well. OxyClean works great to clean glass and for getting labels and glue off of beer bottles by soaking over night in OxyClean and water.

Note: DO NOT use OxyClean for any aluminum.

Powdered Brewery Wash (PBW) is comparable to OxyClean yet is easier to rinse although costs more. When using on stainless steel and copper PBW is not as abrasive.

Another equipment cleaner is dishwasher detergent (Calgonite). Make sure any dishwasher detergent you use is absent of fragrance, color or dye and does not include a rinse aid. Dishwashing detergent is excellent and less expensive than some other methods.

DO NOT use regular dish soap for cleaning your home brewing equipment.

Sanitizing

Sanitizing, sanitization or sanitation is the procedure of killing nearly all microorganisms that could be on your making equipment. Most hobbyists use sanitizing solutions for this process. Because sanitizing cannot abolish microorganisms concealed in dirt or residue you must clean equipment before sanitizing.

Sterilization

Sterilization is when all living cells are killed, such as by heat when boiling. When your equipment has been properly cleaned and sanitized, sterilization is typically not needed for the home brewing process.

Boiling the wort sanitizes the wort. Although when the wort cools sanitation precautions must be taken to make certain your brew stays safe until it is drank. This is why every bit of equipment that has any contact with your brew must be sanitized including your carboys, buckets, spoons, bottles, stirrers, racking cane, bottling wand, auto siphon, stoppers, airlocks, caps, kegs and everything that can or will come in contact with your wort. This includes washing your hands before you touch these items.

Sanitizers for Beer Brewing Equipment

Some home brewers use either bleach or vinegar to sanitize their equipment. When bleach is used all equipment must be thoroughly rinsed before use. Bleach can ruin your clothes, floor, carpet and brew. Rinsing bleach with tap water is not recommended. A no rinse sanitizer is superior to bleach.

NOTE: DO NOT mix bleach and vinegar as they create a toxic gas that can be fatal. You can use one or the other although never both of them.

There are better choices for sanitizing that include Star San, One Step, and Iodorphor.

Most beer brewing kits include a sanitizer and many have One Step. One Step is better for cleaning than sanitizing.

Iodorphor is made with iodine and is available at brewery or farm or livestock stores. Iodorphor can stain some equipment and your skin when not diluted properly.

Star San is perhaps the most accepted sanitizer. This is a no rinse sanitizer that will not affect your beer. Star San comes concentrated and requires mixing with distilled water in a spray bottle.

Star San creates foam that can infiltrate the tight spots on equipment. The foam sticks on equipment and breaks apart in the wort. Star San continues to sanitize when sugar is present and even supplies nutrients for yeast. The manufacturer's instructions plainly state that Star San is a no rinse sanitizer and the foam can stay on your equipment.

NOTE: Always dilute Star San as instructed as the concentration can scratch glass like carboys.

Summary

Clean brewing equipment makes clean beer, and clean beer always tastes better. Home brewing requires diligent sanitizing, which is not just cleaning. *Purportedly, the number one cause for poor tasting beer is poor sanitation.*

Brewing equipment must be cleaned before sanitizing to eliminate residue that harbors germs and bacteria.

Proper cleaning is imperative to good sanitation.

- Cleaning is generally defined as a visible process of removing residue and dirt.
- Sanitizing is the procedure of killing nearly all microorganisms that could be on your making equipment.
- Sterilization is when all living cells are killed, such as by heat when boiling. Boiling the wort sanitizes the wort. Although when the wort cools sanitation precautions must be taken to make certain your brew stays safe until it is drank.

Some home brewers use either bleach or vinegar to sanitize their equipment. When bleach is used all equipment must be thoroughly rinsed before use. Bleach can ruin your clothes, floor, carpet and brew. Rinsing bleach with tap water is not recommended. A no rinse sanitizer is superior to bleach.

Home Brewing

NOTE: DO NOT mix bleach and vinegar as they create a toxic gas that can be fatal.

The best choices for sanitizing include Star San, One Step, and Iodorphor.

7. Partial Mash Beer Brewing

Partial mash beer brewing is the level between extract brewing and all grain brewing. Partial mash beer brewing is also called mini mash brewing. Partial mash brewing goes beyond merely steeping grains due to adding grains to the steep. If you use base malts and specialty grains together they must be mashed. They are not steeped together.

Specialty grains are great for steeping as they have previously been mashed. This means sugars for fermenting have been extracted. Base malts have not yet had sugars extracted. The process of mashing is what extracts those sugars. Partial mash is different from all grain brewing because this process still involves malt extract.

If you can brew tea then you can steep grains for home brewing. Steeping, partial mash and mashing are steps in the process of home brewing that lead to all grain home brewing. In spite of the fact that each style is a progressive step toward all grain brewing, many brewers do not move ahead but find a place in the process they are comfortable and stick there for their brewing.

Mashing is a process that converts grains into sugars to feed the yeast to make beer and injects color and flavor. You have more ingredients to choose.

Steeping involves specialty grains already mashed. The how water extracts color and flavor just like when steeping tea. While mashing adds fermentable sugars, steeping does not.

Do not boil the water when steeping grains. Most brewers use water with a temperature of about 155 degrees F. Boiling releases flavors from tannins in the grains that can negatively affect your final beer. Do not use starchy grains or malts for steeping. Too much starch will can ruin your beer.

The **specialty grains** for steeping are the opposite of the base grains for mashing. The base grains still need to be mashed.

Recipes require different temperatures usually somewhere between 150 degrees F to 165 degrees F. Do not go over degrees F as this can cause bitter beer from the extraction of tannins from the grains.

Hot Steeping: This is the method used most in home brewing. Water is heated to 160 degrees (not boiling) and the grains are allowed to soak for about half an hour at this temperature.

Boil Steeping: This method combines boiling and steeping into one step. **You do not boil the grain**s. The grains are added to brew pot *previous to heating* and *removed before* the temperature gets to 170 degrees F. Then the wort continues to heat. Boil steeping might save time but is less effective than hot steeping.

Cold Steeping: For brewers who wish to steep their grains longer with cold steeping they place them in cold or room temperature water for up to 24 hours.

A lot of brewers will use a mesh bag for the grains when steeping. They fill the bag and drop that in the pot.

Other brewers pour grains directly in the pot and then use a sanitized colander by putting the colander into the brew pot and pouring in the steep filtering the grains out. If using a mesh bag, you can compress the bag to produce more flavor however, be careful as this can also extract tannins.

Using base malts in steeping requires some adjustments to be mashing instead of steeping. Otherwise the starches will not be converted to sugars. There are many malts (and adjuncts) covered in the next chapter to exercise your creativity for producing flavors and colors.

8. All Grain Beer Brewing

When you have some experience extract or partial mash brewing you will be better prepared for all grain brewing. All grain brewing requires additional equipment, attention to math, the right water amounts for mashing and sparging, and temperature, and more steps in the process. You will have more control over your beer and more opportunities for ingredients and flavor. Accuracy will help you run and efficient process and produce better beer.

Brewing all grain beer is the higher level on the difficult scale because this is a more complex process than extract beer brewing. You need additional equipment than for extract brewing.

Home Brewing

There are all kinds setups used to brew all grain beer. They go from simple and inexpensive to sophisticated and costly. There are ready to go brewing systems that range in price from one to five thousand dollars.

Here is a basic equipment list for brewing all grain beer:

- Brew Pot (13 gallon)
- Brew Pot (5-8 gallon)
- Propane Burner2
- Lauter Tun
- Metal Stirring Spoon
- Mash Paddle
- 2 Floating Dairy Thermometers
- Hydrometer and test tube
- Plastic Funnel
- Strainer
- Hop Bags
- Grain Bags
- Wort Chiller or tub of ice

As with the kits and partial mash brewing instead of starting with malt extract, you make malt extract. Because most of the beer taste is attributed to the malt making your own extract presents you with more control over the malt profile of your beer. All grain brewing, the next level up from partial mash brewing, gives you complete control.

Home Brewing

In all grain brewing you will make your own malt extract. Your malt extract will not be the same as the extract you used with a kit or in extract brewing. That extract was condensed to a thick liquid form.

All grain brewing steps:

1. First you choose a grain in an exact weighed out amount.
2. Then add the grain to a specific quantity of water at a targeted temperature.
3. Grains contain starches and this process will convert them to sugars.
4. Then you sparge hot water over the wet grains to gather the sugars. This overflow is called wort.
5. After sparging the rest of the process including boiling, adding hops, and cooling the wort is much the same as extract brewing except all grain brewing often produce more wort.

All grain home brewing takes a while longer than extract brewing. After cleaning and sanitizing all equipment an all grain batch can take eight to ten hours to brew.

Mashing

Mashing is soaking grains to draw out the flavor, fermentable sugars, and color. While mashing and steeping are basically the same process, the fundamental differences are:

- Mashing adds fermentable sugars to the wort where steeping does not.
- You use specialty grains that have been mashed for steeping.
- Mashing uses base malts that require mashing.

Steeping base malts would add starches to the wort which would greatly affect the taste, quality, and clarity of your beer.

Base malts and specialty malts can be combined with some planning for converting the starches into sugars. This can be done as a partial mash or full mash.

Again the difference between partial mashing and all grain brewing is the fact you use malt extract in partial mashing and with all grain brewing you do not use any extract you mash all your base malts from grains.

Mashing requires certain constant temperatures for exact periods to convert starches into sugars. Mashing takes longer than steeping   Constant temperature is the other important factor. Mashing can be done in a special mash tun or lauter tun or you can make your own out of a cooler.

While there are different mashes the typical mash is the single infusion method. This is heating water to a specific temperature usually form 150 degrees F to 165 degrees F. A common temperature is 154 degrees F. Heat the water to a temperature higher than your desired mash temperature (this is called the strike water temperature.) Then when the grains are put in the water the temperature should be close to your target.

[4]Strike water temperature formula:

$$\text{Strike Water Temperature} = (.2/R)(T2-T1) + T2.$$

R is the ratio of water to grain in quarts per pound,

T1 is the grain temperature (Fahrenheit)

T2 is the target mash temperature (Fahrenheit)

Hitting the target mash temperature can be difficult and take practice.

Sparging

The sparge begins after you clarify the wort with a process called vorlauf. Draw several quarts of wort from the tun

---

[4] Palmer, John; "How To Brew"

after mashing; then slowly poured this back into the tun without upsetting the grain bed. When your wort is clear (free of particles and grain,) the vorlauf is complete.

Sparging is the next step after mashing. Sparging is the procedure of rinsing the grain bed to pull out the fermentable sugars from the grains. At the same time you want to avoid extracting bittering tannins from the grain husks.

Sparging is generally accomplished in the mash tun. You can mash and sparge in the same vessel or transfer the grains to a lauter tun. Remember a lauter tun has a false, screened bottom to collect the wort created when you pour the sparge water over the grains.

There are two methods of sparging for home brewing called batch sparging and fly sparging. Fly sparging is usually more efficient although batch sparging is easier. The tun you use also affects efficiency. Round coolers are better for preferred for fly sparging as the false bottoms are round.

Batch Sparging

Batch sparging is the traditional process. The grains are repeatedly rinsed in the mash or lauter tun in batch sparging. Sparge water is added to the tun, time allowed for the grains to settle and the water is drained. This drain is called the "first running." This was repeated several times.

Now home brewers use half the prepared sparge water for the first rinse or running, and the remainder for one last rinse.

Fly Sparging

With fly sparging the wort is drained and water is added at the same rate keeping the grain submerged the whole time. This is done slowly to get as much sugar from the grains as possible. You must also watch for compacted grain that thwarts the runoff and called "stuck sparge." Make sure the water is running over all the grain and not draining through a few channels.
Heat five to seven gallons of water in a separate pot to 170 degrees. This is referred to as the sparge water. Usually you want one and a half times the water for sparging as you used for mashing.

The sparge water is poured over the grain bag or over the grains in a colander or mash tun. Again when batch sparging, the water is poured into the tun and you wait for the grains to settle before and then drain. When fly sparging, the wort is gradually drained and sparge water at the same rate as runoff.

Sparge water temperature is a critical factor because at higher temperatures sugars become more soluble and are easier to extract; 170F degrees is the recommended high temperature. Anything hotter can cause the cause the tannins to be more soluble which can result in a bitter brew.

There are countless other methods to achieve flavor and sugar extraction.

Sparging and PH

Monitor the pH of your wort when fly sparging. If pH is too high, you might extract tannins from the grains, and get a bitter beer. Fly sparging can require acidifying for counteracting any high pH.

In batch sparging the grains are continuously being diluted so pH is not a concern.

The Boil

After sparging is done the remaining process is much the same as extract brewing. There will be more wort and you will need to add hops, cool the wort, and pitch the yeast.

Like extract brewing the wort must be continuously stirred. Keep an eye on the clock and so you know when to add hops. Monitor the boil and stir every few minutes.

Maintaining the right mash temperature is a key to success with the boil. Using the proper amount of water is also imperative.

You need one to one and one fourth quarts of water per pound of grain for mashing. Sparging requires about a half gallon of water per pound of grain. You then boil the wort until you reach the target volume.

Cooling the Wort

After boiling the wort you need to cool quickly. You can do this by moving the brew kettle to tub or large cooler of ice or a much easier method is to invest in a wort chiller.

You need to get your wort to 75 degrees F and you use tap water with a wort chiller. If your tap water is not cold enough, you might need a double wort chiller. The double wort chiller has and additional copper tubing coil. One coil is for the brew kettle. The second coil is for plastic bucket with ice.

After the wort cools to the desired pitching temperature, you then rack the beer to the primary fermenter and pitch the yeast.

Pitching the Yeast

Fermentation begins with the pitching of the yeast. This is nothing more than adding the yeast to the cooled wort. Conditional on what type of yeast you are using, there are different steps to prepare the yeast.

The wort temperature must be below 80 degrees F and aerated before you pitch the yeast. Anything hotter can kill the yeast. Take a specific gravity reading before you pitch the yeast. Most kits include yeast that is ready to go.

Liquid yeast must first make a starter for the yeast before pitching. For partial mash and all grain full boils, pitching requires a couple additional steps to happen before you can add the yeast. For all grain brewing the spent grains and hops must be strained off. Cool and strain the wort. Wort must be cooled quickly to avoid infection and bacteria.

When the wort is in the fermenter and cool now the wort must be aerated. This is when the yeast needs oxygen. You can introduce oxygen into the wort by:

- If doing a partial boil, the wort is aerated by topping off the water.
- Pouring the wort in the fermenter agitates the brew and it gets oxidized.
- Stirring the wort with a large spoon for several minutes gets oxygen in the liquid.
- Shaking the fermenter vigorously for several minutes.
- You can also connect sterilized tubing to an aquarium pump and pump air into the wort.

Brewing in a Bag BIAG

If you have limited space for home brewing such as an apartment, or a small indoor stove that lacks the power to boil large amounts of water, you can brew in a bag (BIAB.) Brewing in a bag is a simplified version of all grain brewing. Everything can be done in one pot. When BIAB you do not need any additional equipment to all grain brew. You can get material called voile and make your own bag or buy one. BIAB home brewing technique is from Australia. With the BIAB method you brew an entire all grain batch in one boil in one pot.

Summary

All grain brewing requires additional equipment, attention to math, the right water amounts for mashing and sparging, and temperature, and more steps in the process. You will have more control over your beer and more opportunities for ingredients and flavor. Accuracy will help you run and efficient process and produce better beer.

Basic equipment list for brewing all grain beer:

- Brew Pot (13 gallon)
- Brew Pot (5-8 gallon)
- Propane Burner2
- Lauter Tun
- Metal Stirring Spoon
- Mash Paddle
- 2 Floating Dairy Thermometers
- Hydrometer and test tube
- Plastic Funnel
- Strainer
- Hop Bags
- Grain Bags
- Wort Chiller or tub of ice

In all grain brewing you will make your own malt extract.

All grain brewing steps:

1. First you choose a grain in an exact weighed out amount.
2. Then add the grain to a specific quantity of water at a targeted temperature.
3. Grains contain starches and this process will convert them to sugars.
4. Then you sparge hot water over the wet grains to gather the sugars. This overflow is called wort.
5. After sparging the rest of the process including boiling, adding hops, and cooling the wort is much the same as extract brewing except all grain brewing often produce more wort.

All grain home brewing takes a while longer than extract brewing. After cleaning and sanitizing all equipment an all grain batch can take eight to ten hours to brew.

Mashing is soaking grains to draw out the flavor, fermentable sugars, and color. While mashing and steeping are basically the same process, the fundamental differences are:

- Mashing adds fermentable sugars to the wort where steeping does not.
- You use specialty grains that have been mashed for steeping.

- Mashing uses base malts that require mashing.

Mashing takes longer than steeping

[5]Strike water temperature formula:

Strike Water Temperature = (.2/R)(T2-T1) + T2.

R is the ratio of water to grain in quarts per pound,

T1 is the grain temperature (Fahrenheit)

T2 is the target mash temperature (Fahrenheit)

Hitting the target mash temperature can be difficult and take practice.

The **sparge** begins after you clarify the wort with a process called **vorlauf**.

Sparging is the next step after mashing.

Batch sparging is the traditional process.

With fly sparging the wort is drained and water is added at the same rate keeping the grain submerged the whole time.

Monitor the pH of your wort when fly sparging. If pH is too high, you might extract tannins from the grains, and get a bitter beer. Fly sparging can require acidifying for counteracting any high pH.

_____

[5] Palmer, John; "How To Brew"

Home Brewing

In batch sparging the grains are continuously being diluted so pH is not a concern.

After sparging is done the remaining process is much the same as extract brewing.

After boiling the wort you need to cool quickly. You can do this by moving the brew kettle to tub or large cooler of ice or a much easier method is to invest in a wort chiller.

Pitching of the yeast is adding the yeast to the cooled wort.

(BIAB) Brewing in a bag is a simplified version of all grain brewing.

9. Fermenting

Specific Gravity

Specific gravity readings will tell you how much of the available sugars have been converted to alcohol. The hydrometer, mentioned earlier, tells you the density of liquids. The denser the liquid, the higher the hydrometer floats in the liquid.

Specific Gravity (SG) is: the ratio of the density of a particular liquid in comparison to the density of water.

Take a hydrometer reading before fermentation. This is referred to as the Original Gravity (OG). The desired SG is the Final Gravity (FG).

Factors that affect SG include the yeast and the type of beer. The results can tell you your brew's percentage of alcohol content and how efficient your production was.

Take your FG reading near the end of fermentation and this will help you know when fermentation is complete.

When the specific gravity is the same several days in a row, your fermentation is done.

Your SG readings should be within five points of your FG target. When Specific Gravity is off by more than five points you have a stuck fermentation.

Stuck Fermentation

When fermentation stalls this means all of the available sugars have not yet been fully converted to CO_2 and alcohol.

Your beer is not ready and bottling this beer can even cause hazardous bottle bombs.

Fermentation stops for several reasons including incorrect temperature or temperature fluctuations.

Remedies include proper temperature maintenance, agitating the fermenter by shaking or rolling, careful stirring, and adding yeast nutrient.

To add yeast nutrient use 3 ounces of corn or table sugar and boil in water. Cool this mix to the target fermentation temperature and add to the beer. Pitching more yeast can also help; using liquid yeast with a starter is recommended.

When nothing seems to be working you can wait this out and let the beer age longer. Avoid using glass bottles for beer that has been in a stuck fermentation period unless resolved.

Primary and Secondary Fermentation

Remember secondary fermentation is not fermentation but aging after completing primary fermentation. Secondary fermentation is for clarifying and conditioning. Allowing beer more time to age makes better beer.

Make sure your beer completely ferments. This can take two weeks or more. Fermentation starts after the yeast has been pitched. There is a lag time for this to begin which can be anywhere from an hour to 72 hours depending on the type and condition of the yeast.

Then beer should be allowed to age after fermentation. This can happen in the fermenter, bottles, or keg.

10. Priming and Bottling Your Beer

When you finish a home brew batch as tempting as tasting your beer might be, your beer will be flat and not yet ready for "prime time." You need to carbonate and bottle your beer and let the aging process happen.

If you are extract brewing with a kit you should have some priming sugar. Otherwise you need to buy some. (This is not regular table sugar.) Calculate the total amount of sugar for your total brew and dissolve that amount in a quart of water. Boil the water until the sugar is all dissolved. Let that blend cool to 70 degrees F, and pour into your bottling bucket before you rack your beer. This process is called Bulk Priming. Here is a list of basic bottling equipment:

- bottling bucket
- siphon tubing
- auto siphon
- racking cane
- bottling wand bottles (at least 50 12 oz bottles)
- bottle caps
- bottle capper

Home Brewing

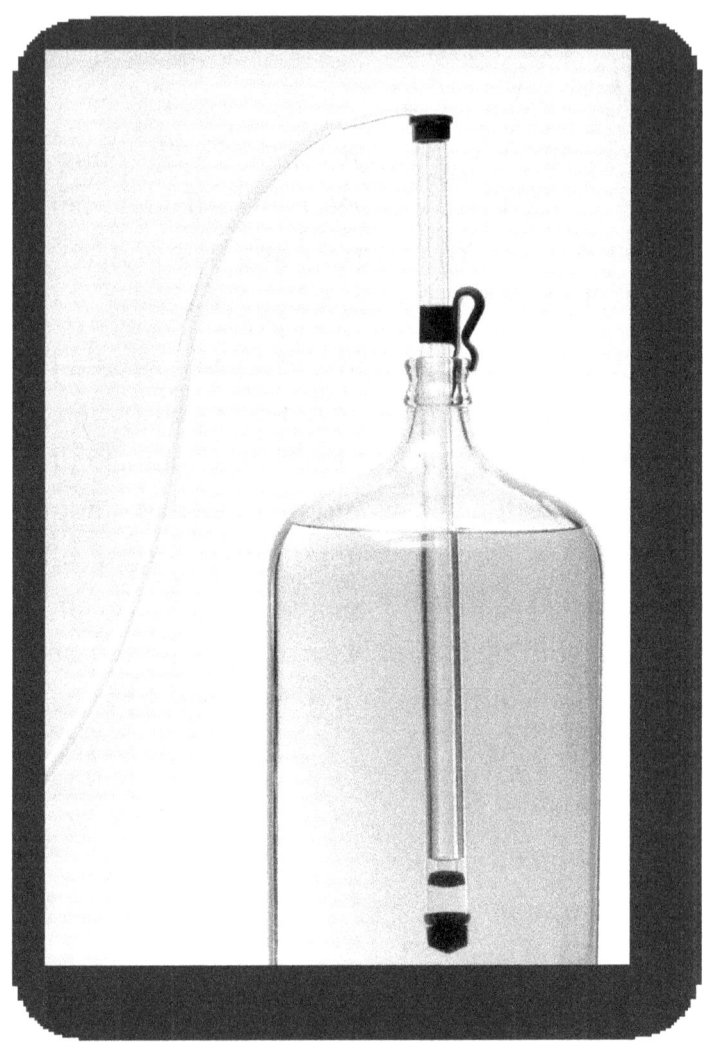

Image Source: http://www.fermtech.ca/

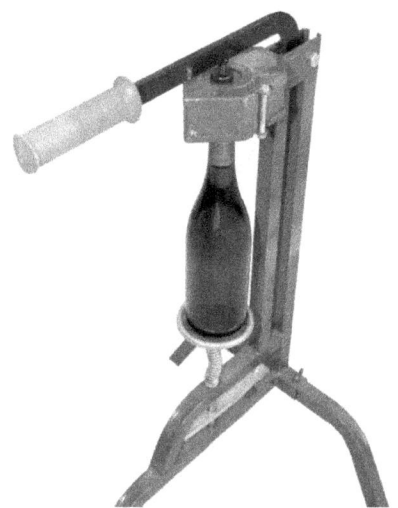

Beer Bottle Cappers

A beer bottle capper seals caps on beer bottles. While there have been many manufacturers of cappers over the years and you can find used cappers, some being antiques, today there are three that are the most popular for home brewers. These include the Red Baron, the Black Beauty, and the Super Agata Bottle Bench Capper.

The Red Baron Capper

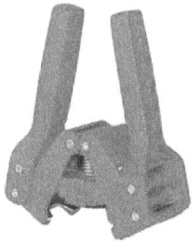

Image Source: www.homebrewers.com

The Red Baron is competitively priced capper with a double lever pull down and magnet to hold the caps. This one uses the standard 26 millimeter bottle caps and can also use a replaceable bell for 29mm caps. The Red Baron is now made with mostly red nylon plastic yet is durable and found in home brewing catalogs and kits.

The Black Beauty Bottle Capper

Image Source: www.love2brew.com

The Black Beauty Capper is much like the Red Baron. They work the same way and the quality is about the same. You cannot use 29mm caps but home brewers do not need them.

Home Brewing

The Super Agata Bottle Bench Capper

Image Source: www.homebrewers.com

The Super Agata Bench Capper uses the 26mm standard caps and can adjustable for the European 29mm caps. You can mount this one to a counter top or work bench and adjust the capper for different bottle heights. A single lever pull down action is faster and easier than the Red Baron or Black Beauty.

Auto Siphon

An auto siphon or wand are not required but make bottling easier. Make sure you clean and sanitize all equipment.

After adding sugar water to the bottling bucket you then add your beer from the fermenter. This should be done with care to avoid splashing which can cause more oxygen in your beer which can result in contamination. Your beer will carbonate in about 3 weeks at a constant temperature out of any light.

Bottling Wand

A bottle wand eliminates the need to siphon. While you do not need a bottling wand to bottle your brew, a bottle wand makes leaving just the right amount of headspace in bottles easier and helps avoid excessive splashing that can contaminate your beer. You attach tubing to the spigot (get a spigot if you do not have one on your bottling bucket) and the bottling wand and place the wand on the bottom of the bottle. Filling your bottles from the bottom up allows you to get the right amount of headspace for carbonation.

You can sanitize your bottles by placing them upside down in a dishwasher. Wash them with a full cycle without soap.

WARNING: If you use bottling wand leave airspace in the bottle or you could create a bottle bombs. The pressure from the CO_2 (carbonation) needs some space.

Kegs

Using kegs has some advantages compared to bottling:

- You save time kegging because every bottle must be cleaned and sanitized,
- Bottles can be more difficult to store. A five gallon home brew batch will fill 50 bottles that are 12 ounces each.
- Bottles all must be capped which requires caps and a capper.
- Racking your beer to a keg is easier than bottling. You can purge the keg with CO2 before racking to get rid of all the oxygen (not required.)

You can rack your beer from the fermenter into the keg. The beer can be primed for several weeks in the keg or use a CO2 tank for forced carbonation. Then your beer is ready in a few days. When you use CO2 and a keg you can control the amount of carbonation which you cannot do with bottles.

Home Brewing

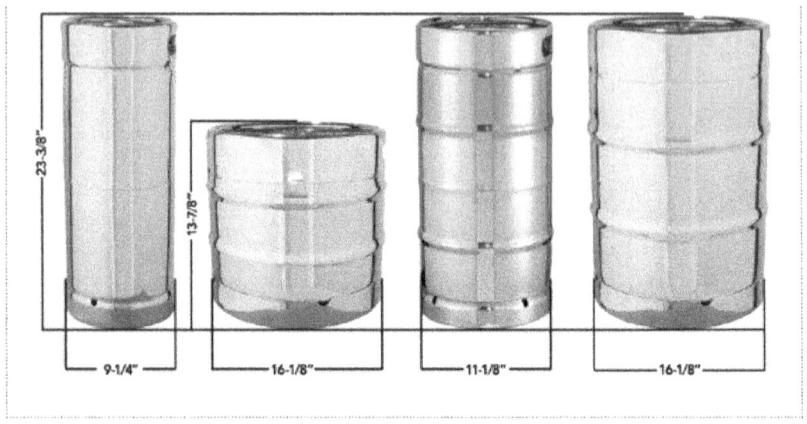

AKA	Cylinder	Pony Keg	¼ Barrel	Full-Size Keg
Gallons	5- 5.16	7.75	7.75	15.50
Ounces	661	992	992	1984
# of 12 oz. beers	55	82	82	165
Weight (Full)	58 Pounds	87 Pounds	87 Pounds	161 Pounds

Image Source: drunkentailgate.com

Home Brewing Equipment for Kegging

You need a place to store the kegs such as a kegerator or you can convert a freezer or fridge. Home brewers spend a few hundred to a thousand dollars depending on what they choose but this is a one-time expense whereas bottling requires purchasing bottles and caps every time you brew.

You can still bottle beer when desired.

You also need a CO_2 tank and regulator for carbonation. A regulator helps you control the pressure and temperature. Hoses and fittings are needed to connect the CO_2 tank to the kegs and faucets. You also need a tap for dispensing your beer. There are options such as a tower tap system or less expensive picnic or party tap.

Transferring Beer to a Keg

You need a tube that will reach to the bottom of your keg when racking. You want to keep the end of the tube submerged to steer clear of splashing and aerating. After the transfer replace the sanitized keg lid and seal. Then you need to purge the headspace in the keg of any oxygen with CO_2 before pressurizing.

You can get kegs with pressure relief valves that help you do this. Allow CO_2 to flow into the keg for 20 to 30 seconds with the pressure release valve open; after that shut the gas off. If you do not have a release valve on your keg let the lid remain unsealed to allow the keg to vent.

Then you will be ready to carbonate your beer.

Forced carbonation is the process of connecting your CO_2 tank to your keg and then blowing gas in. If you lay the keg horizontally while you do this there will be more surface area and subsequently better carbonation. When you can no longer here any bubbling coming from within the keg you are done.

Home Brewing

	PSI (Pounds Per Square Inch)																													
	1	2	3	4	5	6	7	8	9	10	11	12	13	14	15	16	17	18	19	20	21	22	23	24	25	26	27	28	29	30
30°F	1.82	1.92	2.03	2.14	2.23	2.36	2.48	2.60	2.70	2.82	2.93	3.02	3.13	3.24	3.35	3.46	3.57	3.67	3.78	3.89	4.00	4.11	4.22	4.33	4.44	4.66	4.77	4.87	4.98	4.98
31°F	1.78	1.88	2.00	2.10	2.20	2.31	2.42	2.54	2.65	2.76	2.86	2.96	3.07	3.17	2.28	3.39	3.50	3.60	3.71	3.82	3.93	4.03	4.14	4.25	4.35	4.46	4.57	4.68	4.78	4.89
32°F	1.75	1.85	1.95	2.05	2.15	2.27	2.38	2.48	2.59	2.70	2.80	2.90	3.00	3.11	3.21	3.31	3.42	3.52	3.63	3.73	3.84	3.94	4.04	4.15	4.25	4.36	4.46	4.57	4.67	4.77
33°F	1.71	1.81	1.91	2.01	2.10	2.23	2.33	2.43	2.53	2.63	2.74	2.84	2.96	3.06	3.15	3.25	3.35	3.46	3.56	3.66	3.76	3.87	3.97	4.07	4.18	4.28	4.38	4.48	4.59	4.69
34°F	1.68	1.78	1.86	1.97	2.06	2.18	2.28	2.38	2.48	2.58	2.69	2.79	2.90	3.00	3.09	3.19	3.29	3.39	3.49	3.59	3.69	3.79	3.90	4.00	4.10	4.20	4.30	4.40	4.50	4.60
35°F	1.63	1.73	1.83	1.93	2.02	2.14	2.24	2.34	2.43	2.52	2.63	2.73	2.83	2.93	3.02	3.12	3.22	3.32	3.42	3.52	3.62	3.72	3.82	3.92	4.01	4.11	4.21	4.31	4.41	4.51
36°F	1.60	1.69	1.79	1.88	1.98	2.09	2.19	2.29	2.38	2.47	2.57	2.67	2.77	2.86	2.96	3.05	3.15	3.24	3.34	3.43	3.53	3.63	3.72	3.82	3.92	4.01	4.11	4.21	4.31	4.41
37°F	1.55	1.65	1.74	1.84	1.94	2.04	2.14	2.24	2.33	2.42	2.52	2.62	2.71	2.80	2.90	3.00	3.09	3.18	3.27	3.37	3.46	3.56	3.65	3.75	3.84	3.94	4.03	4.13	4.22	4.32
38°F	1.52	1.61	1.71	1.80	1.90	2.00	2.10	2.20	2.29	2.38	2.48	2.57	2.66	2.75	2.85	2.94	3.03	3.12	3.21	3.30	3.40	3.49	3.59	3.68	3.77	3.87	3.96	4.05	4.15	4.24
39°F	1.49	1.59	1.67	1.77	1.86	1.96	2.06	2.15	2.25	2.34	2.43	2.52	2.61	2.70	2.80	2.89	2.98	3.07	3.16	3.25	3.34	3.44	3.53	3.62	3.71	3.81	3.90	3.99	4.08	4.18
40°F	1.47	1.56	1.65	1.74	1.83	1.92	2.01	2.10	2.20	2.30	2.39	2.47	2.56	2.65	2.75	2.84	2.93	3.01	3.10	3.19	3.28	3.37	3.46	3.55	3.64	3.73	3.82	3.91	4.01	4.10
41°F	1.43	1.52	1.61	1.70	1.79	1.88	1.97	2.06	2.16	2.25	2.34	2.43	2.52	2.60	2.70	2.79	2.88	2.96	3.05	3.14	3.23	3.32	3.41	3.50	3.59	3.68	3.77	3.86	3.95	4.04
42°F	1.39	1.48	1.57	1.66	1.75	1.85	1.94	2.02	2.12	2.21	2.30	2.39	2.48	2.56	2.65	2.74	2.83	2.91	3.00	3.09	3.18	3.26	3.35	3.44	3.53	3.62	3.70	3.79	3.88	3.97
43°F	1.37	1.46	1.54	1.63	1.72	1.81	1.90	1.99	2.08	2.17	2.26	2.34	2.43	2.52	2.61	2.69	2.78	2.86	2.95	3.04	3.13	3.21	3.30	3.39	3.47	3.56	3.65	3.74	3.82	3.91
44°F	1.35	1.43	1.52	1.60	1.69	1.78	1.87	1.95	2.04	2.13	2.22	2.30	2.39	2.47	2.56	2.64	2.73	2.81	2.90	2.99	3.07	3.10	3.24	3.33	3.41	3.50	3.58	3.67	3.76	3.84
45°F	1.32	1.41	1.49	1.58	1.66	1.75	1.84	1.91	2.00	2.08	2.17	2.26	2.34	2.42	2.51	2.60	2.69	2.77	2.86	2.94	3.02	3.11	3.19	3.28	3.36	3.45	3.53	3.62	3.70	3.79
46°F	1.28	1.37	1.45	1.54	1.62	1.71	1.80	1.88	1.96	2.04	2.13	2.22	2.30	2.38	2.47	2.55	2.64	2.72	2.81	2.89	2.98	3.06	3.15	3.23	3.31	3.40	3.48	3.57	3.65	3.74
47°F	1.26	1.34	1.42	1.51	1.59	1.68	1.76	1.84	1.92	2.00	2.08	2.26	2.34	2.42	2.50	2.59	2.67	2.76	2.84	2.93	3.02	3.09	3.18	3.26	3.35	3.43	3.51	3.60		
48°F	1.23	1.31	1.39	1.48	1.56	1.65	1.73	1.81	1.89	1.96	2.05	2.14	2.22	2.30	2.38	2.46	2.54	2.62	2.71	2.79	2.88	2.96	3.04	3.13	3.21	3.30	3.38	3.46	3.54	3.63
49°F	1.21	1.29	1.37	1.45	1.53	1.62	1.70	1.79	1.86	1.93	2.01	2.10	2.18	2.25	2.34	2.42	2.50	2.58	2.67	2.75	2.83	2.91	3.00	3.07	3.15	3.23	3.31	3.39	3.47	3.55
50°F	1.18	1.26	1.34	1.42	1.50	1.59	1.66	1.74	1.82	1.90	1.98	2.06	2.14	2.21	2.30	2.38	2.46	2.54	2.62	2.70	2.78	2.86	2.94	3.02	3.10	3.17	3.25	3.33	3.41	3.49
51°F	1.16	1.24	1.32	1.40	1.47	1.55	1.63	1.71	1.79	1.87	1.95	2.02	2.10	2.18	2.26	2.34	2.42	2.49	2.57	2.65	2.74	2.82	2.90	2.97	3.05	3.13	3.19	3.27	3.34	3.42
52°F	1.16	1.23	1.31	1.39	1.46	1.54	1.61	1.68	1.76	1.84	1.92	1.99	2.06	2.14	2.22	2.30	2.38	2.45	2.53	2.61	2.68	2.76	2.84	2.92	3.00	3.06	3.13	3.22	3.30	3.37
53°F	1.14	1.21	1.29	1.36	1.44	1.51	1.59	1.66	1.74	1.81	1.89	1.96	2.03	2.10	2.18	2.26	2.34	2.41	2.49	2.57	2.64	2.71	2.79	2.86	2.94	3.01	3.09	3.16	3.24	3.31
54°F	1.12	1.19	1.27	1.34	1.41	1.49	1.56	1.63	1.71	1.78	1.86	1.93	2.00	2.07	2.15	2.22	2.30	2.37	2.45	2.52	2.59	2.66	2.74	2.81	2.89	2.96	3.04	3.10	3.17	3.24
55°F	1.10	1.17	1.24	1.31	1.39	1.46	1.53	1.60	1.68	1.75	1.82	1.89	1.97	2.04	2.12	2.18	2.26	2.33	2.40	2.47	2.54	2.62	2.69	2.76	2.83	2.89	2.97	3.04	3.11	3.18
56°F	1.07	1.15	1.22	1.29	1.36	1.43	1.50	1.57	1.65	1.72	1.79	1.86	1.93	2.00	2.06	2.15	2.22	2.29	2.36	2.43	2.50	2.57	2.64	2.71	2.78	2.85	2.92	2.99	3.06	3.13
57°F	1.05	1.12	1.19	1.26	1.33	1.40	1.47	1.54	1.61	1.68	1.75	1.81	1.90	1.97	2.04	2.11	2.18	2.25	2.32	2.39	2.46	2.53	2.60	2.66	2.73	2.80	2.87	2.94	3.00	3.08
58°F	1.03	1.10	1.17	1.24	1.30	1.37	1.44	1.51	1.59	1.67	1.74	1.80	1.87	1.94	2.01	2.08	2.15	2.21	2.28	2.35	2.42	2.48	2.55	2.62	2.69	2.75	2.82	2.88	2.95	3.02
59°F	1.02	1.09	1.16	1.22	1.29	1.36	1.43	1.49	1.56	1.64	1.71	1.77	1.84	1.91	1.98	2.04	2.11	2.17	2.24	2.31	2.38	2.43	2.50	2.57	2.64	2.70	2.77	2.84	2.91	2.97
60°F	1.01	1.08	1.15	1.21	1.28	1.34	1.41	1.47	1.54	1.62	1.62	1.75	1.82	1.88	1.95	2.01	2.08	2.14	2.21	2.27	2.34	2.40	2.47	2.53	2.60	2.66	2.73	2.79	2.86	2.92
61°F	0.99	1.05	1.12	1.18	1.24	1.31	1.37	1.44	1.50	1.57	1.63	1.69	1.76	1.82	1.89	1.95	2.02	2.08	2.14	2.21	2.27	2.34	2.40	2.47	2.53	2.59	2.66	2.72	2.79	2.85
62°F	0.96	1.02	1.09	1.15	1.21	1.27	1.34	1.40	1.46	1.52	1.59	1.65	1.71	1.78	1.84	1.90	1.97	2.03	2.09	2.15	2.22	2.28	2.34	2.41	2.47	2.53	2.59	2.66	2.72	2.78
63°F	0.93	0.99	1.06	1.12	1.18	1.24	1.30	1.36	1.42	1.49	1.55	1.61	1.67	1.73	1.79	1.85	1.92	1.98	2.04	2.10	2.16	2.22	2.28	2.35	2.41	2.47	2.53	2.59	2.65	2.71
64°F	0.91	0.97	1.03	1.09	1.15	1.21	1.27	1.33	1.39	1.45	1.51	1.57	1.63	1.69	1.75	1.81	1.87	1.93	1.99	2.05	2.11	2.17	2.23	2.29	2.35	2.41	2.47	2.52	2.58	2.64
65°F	0.88	0.94	1.00	1.06	1.11	1.17	1.23	1.29	1.35	1.41	1.46	1.52	1.58	1.64	1.70	1.76	1.82	1.87	1.93	1.99	2.05	2.11	2.17	2.23	2.28	2.34	2.40	2.46	2.52	2.58

Table Key:
Blue = Under-Carbonated, 0 - 1.40 volumes CO2
Gray = Stouts and porters, 1.50 - 2.20 volumes CO2
Green = Lagers, Ales, Ambers, most beers, 2.20 - 2.60 volumes CO2
Yellow = Highly carbonated ales, Lambics, Wheat beers 2.60 - 4.0 volumes CO2
Red = Over-carbonated (except for certain specialty ales) 4.1+ volumes CO2

* This chart is for use in force carbonating draft beer. Use this force carbonation chart at your own risk. Never exceed the pressure rating of the carbonating vessel as injury to

Images Source: www.goallgrain.com

Carbonation Chart

How much pressure (measured in psi) you need for your beer depends on volume, storage temperature and style of beer. The colder the temperature the less pressure is needed for carbonation.

The carbonation chart shows you the amount of pressure you need for proper carbonation. Set your tank accordingly and in a day or two your beer will be fully carbonated.

Periodically check your lines and fittings for any leaks.

A spray bottle filled with soapy water can help you. Spray the line where you suspect a leak and the sop will bubble at the leak.

Cornelius Kegs Used In Beer Brewing

Cornelieus kegs, also referred to as "corny" kegs are small five gallon kegs. Commercial kegs are 15.5 gallons. Because five gallons is the common batch size for home brewing the Cornelius Kegs hold a batch. They take up less space, cost

Image Source: https://sites.google.com/site/ibrewstuff/

less, are easy to move, and can fit in freezers and small kegerators. There are also used ones available especially from soda distributors and several companies that make these kegs.

These canisters were originally designed for soda for bars and restaurants. Now they have been replaced by soda mixes in plastic bags and an abundance of used Cornelius kegs.

Image Source: https://sites.google.com/site/ibrewstuff/

Corny kegs have two different types of valves, and a ball lock and pin lock. The locks will show the type of hose fittings needed for the valves. Getting two or more kegs can make sure you are ready to brew and keep beer on hand.

DMS

Dimethyl Sulfide (DMS) is a sulfur compound that is produced when beer ferments. This often has a cooked corn smell. DMS (Dimethyl Sulfide) is a byproduct of mashing and fermentation and can greatly affect the taste of the beer. DMS is produced when wort is heated and found in all beer and lagers in particular which is wanted in low levels. If your beer has an odor of cabbage your beer has been infected.

Half of the DMS is boiled off in 40 minute s of a vigorous boil. This is why a boil of 90 minutes or longer is advised. Because the DMS needs to boil off do not cover your pot. Rapidly cooling the wort after boiling can also help prevent DMS conversion.

CO2 bubbles that happen in fermentation also help remove from DMS from your brew. DMS aromas happen during fermentation so do not surmise your beer is bad should you smell them. These smells are most perceivable in lightly flavored beers.

Summary

If you are extract brewing with a kit you should have some priming sugar. (This is not regular table sugar.) Calculate the total amount of sugar for your total brew and dissolve that amount in a quart of water. Boil the water until the sugar is all dissolved. Let that blend cool to 70 degrees F, and pour into your bottling bucket before you rack your beer. This process is called Bulk Priming.

Basic bottling equipment:

- bottling bucket
- siphon tubing
- auto siphon
- racking cane
- bottling wand bottles (at least 50 12 oz bottles)
- bottle caps
- bottle capper

An auto siphon or wand are not required but make bottling easier. Make sure you clean and sanitize all equipment.

A bottle wand eliminates the need to siphon.

WARNING: If you use a bottling wand leave airspace in the bottle or you could create a bottle bombs. The pressure from the CO_2 (carbonation) needs some space.

Kegs: Using kegs has some advantages compared to bottling.

You can rack your beer from the fermenter into the keg. You want to keep the end of the tube submerged to steer clear of splashing and aerating.

You can purge the keg with CO2 before racking to get rid of all the oxygen (not required.) You can get kegs with pressure relief valves that help you do this.

Forced carbonation is the process of connecting your CO2 tank to your keg and then blowing gas in.

Periodically check your lines and fittings for any leaks.

Cornelieus kegs, also referred to as "corny" kegs are small five gallon kegs.

Dimethyl Sulfide (DMS) is a sulfur compound that is produced when beer ferments. If your beer has an odor of cabbage your beer has been infected. Because the DMS needs to boil off do not cover your pot. Rapidly cooling the wort after boiling can also help prevent DMS conversion.

11. Brewing at Home Legalities

Note: Home brewing laws are ever evolving and the following information is subject to change without notice: The information herein is to the best of our knowledge and should not be used as a substitute for legal advice specific to the laws of your country, state, or location.

U.S. Federal Law

Home brewing is federally legal in the U.S. The 18th Amendment to the U.S. Constitution, ratifying prohibition in 1919, made home brewing in the U.S. illegal. The 21st Amendment repealed prohibition in 1933, yet the legislation failed to legalize home beer making (home wine making was legalized at that time).

On October 14, 1978, President Jimmy Carter signed H.R. 1337, which contained an amendment creating an exemption from taxation for beer brewed at home for personal or family use. This exemption went into effect in February 1979.

United States Home Brewing Statutes

Status: Permitted, subject to age restriction and amount (gallonage).

Statute

Home Brewing

United States Code of Federal Regulations Title 27, Part 25, Subpart L, Section 25.205 and Section 25.206

Beer for Personal or Family Use

25.205 Production.

(a) Any adult may produce beer, without payment of tax, for personal or family use and not for sale. An adult is any individual who is 18 years of age or older. If the locality in which the household is located requires a greater minimum age for the sale of beer to individuals, the adult shall be that age before commencing the production of beer. This exemption does not authorize the production of beer for use contrary to State or local law.

(b) The production of beer per household, without payment of tax, for personal or family use may not exceed:

(1) 200 gallons per calendar year if there are two or more adults residing in the household, or

(2) 100 gallons per calendar year if there is only one adult residing in the household.

(c) Partnerships except as provided in §25.207, corporations or associations may not produce beer, without payment of tax, for personal or family use.

25.206 Removal of beer.

Beer made under 25.205 may be removed from the premises where made for personal or family use including use at organized affairs, exhibitions or competitions such as homemaker's contests, tastings or judging. Beer removed under this section may not be sold or offered for sale.

Definitions

Beer: Beer, ale, porter, stout, and other similar fermented beverages (including saké and similar products) of any name or description containing one-half of one percent or more of alcohol by volume, brewed or produced from malt, wholly or in part, or from any substitute for malt. Standards for the production of beer appear in 25.15.

State Laws

The 21st Amendment leaves regulation of alcohol and home brewing to the states. Some states have specific laws and others have less definition. Some state outlaw transportation of home brewed alcohol and others permit transportation to specific events.

Sales Tax

Many states in the U.S. have varying laws regarding sales tax for home brewing equipment and supplies.

Example: Wisconsin

Home Beer Brewing Ingredients, Equipment, and Supplies

Ingredients

[6]Certain products used to make beer are a "food or food ingredient" and qualify for exemption from Wisconsin sales and use tax. Examples of items exempt from Wisconsin sales and use tax when used in the home brewing of beer for personal consumption include:

- Malts - extracts, powders, grains

- Unmalted grains - corn, rice, barley, rye, wheat, oats

- Adjuncts - corn and rice powders or syrups, honey

- Hops - leaf, pellets, frozen, and extracts

- Maltodextrine

- Priming sugars - corn sugar, cane sugar, and "candi" sugars, except "candi" sugars sold in the form of bars, drops, or pieces, which are taxable as the sale of a food or food ingredient that is "candy"

- Flavorings - extracts, herbs, and botanicals

---

[6] http://www.revenue.wi.gov/taxpro/news/120221.html

Home Brewing

- Lactose

- Brewing yeast - liquid or dried

- Distilled water

- Fruit juice - must be more than 50% fruit juice by volume to be exempt. If less than 50% fruit juice by volume, it is taxable as a soft drink.

- Water chemicals - calcium carbonate, Epsom salts, gypsum, non-iodized salt, burtonisation salts, phosphoric acid, lactic acid. If the product is labeled for sale with a "supplement (al) facts box" on the packaging, it is taxable as a food or food ingredient that is a "dietary supplement."

Equipment and Supplies

Sales of equipment and supplies such as brewing pots, plastic buckets, carboys, fermentation locks, thermometers, wort chillers, siphon tubes, plastic hoses, bottles, bottle caps, bottle cappers, and beer labels are taxable. Supplies used or consumed in making and storing the beer, such as cleaners, sanitizers are also taxable.

Clarifiers and fining agents such as Irish moss, bentonite, and polyclar that are used to filter the beer during the home brewing process are also taxable. Although some clarifiers and fining agents may be ingested or chewed, they do not qualify for the exemption from Wisconsin sales and use tax for food and food ingredients because they are not ingested or chewed for their taste or nutritional value.

Home Beer Brewing Kits

Home beer brewing kits that contain a combination of taxable and nontaxable products (i.e., equipment and supplies and food and food ingredients) and sold for a single non-itemized price are subject to Wisconsin sales and use tax if more than 50% of the seller's sales price and purchase price of the products contained in the kit relates to the taxable products. If 50% or less of the seller's sales price or purchase price of the products contained in the kit relates to the taxable products, the entire selling price of the home beer brewing kit is exempt from Wisconsin sales and use tax.

Home Brewing Laws by Country

Home brewing laws are ever evolving and the following information is subject to change without notice:

[7]**Australia:** Legal for personal consumption if a still is not used.

Canada: Legal in most Canadian provinces.

Czech Republic: Legal with a limit of 200 Liters per household per year of beer.

Germany: Legal. 200 liters of beer per household per year may be produced without taxation and notification of the local customs office is required.

Hungary: Legal. 1000 liters of beer per person per year may be produced without taxation.

Poland: Legal for personal use only.

Sweden: Legal for personal use only.

Ireland: Legal for personal use only.

Russian Federation: Legal for personal use only.

Finland: Legal for personal use only.

Norway: Legal for personal use only.

---

[7] https://en.wikipedia.org/wiki/Homebrewing

United Kingdom: Legal in unlimited quantity for personal use only.

United States: Legal. States remain regulate home brewing. Most states permit 100 gallons of home brew beer per adult per year for personal use only.

New Zealand: Legal for personal use only.

South Africa: Legal for personal use only.

Singapore: Legal up to 30 liters per household per month for personal use only. .

Hong Kong: Legal.

Japan: Legal up to 1% alcohol by volume only.

Malaysia: Illegal

Iran: Illegal

India: Illegal

Eritrea: Legal

Ethiopia: Legal

Sudan: Legal

Appendix

Alcohol Beverage Control Agency
Alcohol and Tobacco Tax and Trade Bureau
Public Information Officer
1310 G Street, NW., Suite 300
Washington, D.C. 20220
Phone: 202.453.2000

Home Brew Clubs

Australia

Blood, Sweat & Beers
Brisbane 4500
Phone: (073) 495-8131
Email: john@occskills.com.au

Brisbane Amateur Beer Brewers
Brisbane, Queensland 4121
Phone: +61733436484
Email: info@babbrewers.com
www.babbrewers.com/

PUBS
Brisbane 4503
Phone: (613) 886-2727
Email: pubsbrewclub@yahoo.com.au

The GoldCLUB
Buckfield, ME 4220
Phone: (042) 097-5877
Email: thegoldclub@digitaldirtdesign.com
www.facebook.com/pages/The-GoldCLUB/387980561281381

IBUs (Illawarra Brewers Union)
Bulli, NSW 2516
Phone: 610242858663
Email: ray@ibunion.org
ibunion.org

Macarthur Ale and Lager Enthusiasts
Campbelltown, NSW 2560
Email: itslinz@gmail.com
au.groups.yahoo.com/group/Macarthur_Ale_and_Lager_Enthusiasts/

Canberra Brewers Club
Canberra, ACT 2601
Phone: +61 417 692 211
Email: president@canberrabrewers.org
www.canberrabrewers.org/

Home Brewing

Bayside Brewers Club
Chelsea, Victoria 3195
Email: future@alphalink.com.au

Northside Wine/Beermakers Circ
Frenchs Forest, NSW 2086

Amateur Brewers Of Victoria
Glen Waverly
Phone: 561-4603

Western Sydney Brewers
Parramatta, NSW
Phone: +61 423276241
Email: joshb78@gmail.com
www.westernsydneybrewers.com

West Coast Brewers
Perth, W. Australia 6000
Phone: 08 9419 7699
Email: Admin@westcoastbrewers.com
www.westcoastbrewers.com

Hills Brewers Guild
Sydney, NSW 2151
Email: chris.lynch@ozemail.com.au
www.hillsbrewersguild.com

Redwood Coast Brewers
Tamworth 2340
Phone: (616) 766-7852

Canada

Cowtown Yeast Wranglers
Calgary, AB T3E 7J3
Email: info@yeastwranglers.ca
www.yeastwranglers.ca

Calgary Homebrewers Association
Calgary, AB T2H 0C2
Phone: (403) 264- 2703
Email: beer@calgaryhomebrew.ca
www.calgaryhomebrew.ca

Brewshiners of Georgian Bay
Collingwood, ON L9Y 3Z2
Phone: (705) 445-1087
Email: highlander5@sympatico.ca

Edmonton Homebrewers Guild
Edmonton, AB T6E 0C7
Phone: 451-7633
Email: roxanneih@shaw.ca
www.ehg.ca

The Brewnosers
Halifax, Nova Scotia
Phone: 902-483-6420
Email: admin@brewnosers.org
www.brewnosers.org

HOZER (Hamilton Ontario Zymurgy Enthusiast Ring)
Hamilton, ON L8P 2E8
Phone: 905-393-7900
Email: hozer.ca@gmail.com
www.hozer.ca

London Homebrewers Guild
London, Ontario N6G4Z4
Phone: (519) 671-5139

Home Brewing

Email: info@londonbrewers.ca
www.londonbrewers.ca

BeerShack Brewers
Mississauga, ON L4T 2A5
Phone: (416) 937-9872
Email: lou@beershack.ca
www.beershack.ca

Brasseurs Amateur Réunis
Montréal, Québec H1E2P6
Phone: (450) 812-4445
Email: BAR.Montreal.info@gmail.com
clubdebrasseursmaison.weebly.com

Amateur Winemaker /Mr. Paul Jean Jr.
Ottawa, ON K2B 8S5
Phone: (613) 825-3229
Email: jeanpaul@igs.net

Ale & Lager Enthusiasts of Saskatchewan
Regina, SK S4X 2T1
Phone: (306)525-2245
Email: exec@alesclub.com
www.alesclub.com

Saskatoon Berry Brewers
Saskatoon, SK S7N 3S8
Phone: (306) 966-7822
Email: Robert.Schultz@usask.ca
www.usask.ca/~alexson/sbbhp.htm

Saskatoon Headhunters
Saskatoon, SK S7N 4M9
Email: nacht@sasktel.net

Thunder Bay Home Brewers Assn.
Thunder Bay, ON P7A 8A1
Phone: (201) 568-5336

Southern Ontario Brewers (SOBs)
Toronto, ON
Email: thatleetboybrews@gmail.com

UBC Brewing Club
Vancouver, BC
Email: ubcbrewingclub@gmail.com
brubc.ca/

VanBrewers
Vancouver, BC
Phone: (604) 209-4976
Email: admin@vanbrewers.ca
www.vanbrewers.ca

Meadworks Brewing Club
Vancouver, BC V6K 2L8
Phone: (604) 731-5359
Email: kelly@meadworks.ca
www.meadworks.ca

Campaign for Real Ale
Victoria, BC V8X 5E1
Phone: (250) 595-7728

BrewVIC
Victoria, BC
Phone: (250) 598-5175
Email: club@brewvic.ca
www.brewvic.com

Winnipeg Brew Bombers
Winnipeg, MB R2G 2X5

Phone: (204) 667-8021
Email: secretary@winnipegbrewbombers.ca

New Zealand

Mainland Brewers
Canterbury 8170
Phone: 03 3181 440
Email: nigel.stephanie@xtra.co.nz

Far North Brewers & Vintners
Mangonui Northland

Hibiscus Winemakers & Brewers
Orewa, Auckland

Massey University Brewing Society (MUBS)
Wellington, N. Island
Email: masseybrewsoc@live.com
facebook.com/masseybrewsoc

United Kingdom

Beeston Beer Circle
Beeston, Notts
Phone: (115) 925-5999

Bristol Brewing Circle
Bristol
Phone: 0117-909-1454
Email: alastair.kocho-williams@uwe.ac.uk
bristolbrewers.wordpress.com/

Bristol Craft Brewers
Bristol BS1 9UD
Phone: (0795) 099-1979
Email: alikocho@googlemail.com
www.bristolcraftbrewers.co.uk/

Scottish Craft Brewers
Dunbar, East Lothian
Email: dell@which.net

The Northern Craft Brewers
Heald Green, Cheshire
Phone: (+44) 7830304929
Email: shane@bridestone.com
www.northerncraftbrewers.co.uk

Broad Ripple Celebration Club
Indianapolis, IN 46220
Phone: (317) 985-5195
Email: wheresnorwaldo@gmail.com

Worshipful Co. Of Brewers
London
Phone: (071) 606-1301

London Amateur Brewers
London N1 7TA
Email: b.fields@gold.ac.uk
londonamateurbrewers.co.uk

Home Brewing

Oxford Brewers Group
Oxford, Oxon OX1 3JS
Email:
will@oxfordbrewers.com
www.oxfordbrewers.com/

United States

There are over 1,000 home brew clubs in the U.S
You can locate a list of the clubs in your state here:
http://www.homebrewersassociation.org/pages/directories/find-a-club

Glossary

A

Adjunct: Unmalted grain for brewing beer. Refers to non fermentable sugars or other ingredients besides water, hops, yeast, and malted grains.

Aerate: Adding air to the wort to supply oxygen for the yeast.

Airlocks: Plastic devices with liquid chambers for the fermenter designed to allow CO2 to be released while keeping air and contaminates out.

Ale - Beer brewed using top fermenting yeast beer.

All Grain: Beer brewing style where extracts are produced from grains.

Attenuation: Measure of the sugars converted into alcohol during fermentation. This is determined by measuring the specific drop in gravity from the original gravity using a hydrometer.

B

Barley: Grain used as the chief source of fermentable sugars and proteins for brewing beer.

Beta Acids: Soft resins harsher in flavor than alpha acids also found in hops.

Bittering Hops: Hops with high amounts of alpha acids that are used to add bitterness to brew during the boil.

Bittering Wort: Wort after the boil and after hops have been added.

Body: The sensation of fullness of beer in the mouth.

Bottle Bombs: Bottles of beer that explode from too much pressure caused by excessive CO_2

Bottling Wand: A metal or stiff plastic tube with a one-way flow valve at the lower end used in bottling.

C

Carboy: Fermentation vessel made of glass or aluminum with a narrow neck.

Conditioning: Secondary fermentation or carbonation of beer depending on the brewing style.

D

Dimethyl Sulfide (DMS) – Sulfur compound that causes a corn smell.

Dry Hopping: Method of hopping to add aroma to beer after wort boiling, usually during secondary fermentation.

E

Extract: Soluble material extracted from barley malt and adjuncts either by the mashing process or the malt extract that comes ion brewing kits.

F

Fermentation: The process where yeast cells convert sugars into carbon dioxide molecule and ethanol.

Final Gravity (FG): The concentration of malt sugar in beer measured after the first fermentation stage is complete.

Finishing Hops: Aromatic hops that give beer aroma and are added during the last 5 minutes of the boil.

H

Hops: Flowers of the humulus lupulus plant used to bitter beer and add flavor and aroma..

Hydrometer: Measures the concentration of malt sugars in the wort.

International Bittering Units: Measurement of the bitterness of beer. One IBU equals one milligram of isomerized alpha acids per liter of beer.

K

Kiln: Furnace used to dry or roast malt.

L

Lager: Style of beer made from the bottom fermenting yeast. This also describes the process of storing beer at low temperatures and for long periods.

Lauter Tun: Vessel for filtering the wort from the grains after the mash.

Lovibond: Unit of measure for the color of malt.

M

Malt Extract: Sweet wort packaged as thick syrup or dry powder in kits.

Maltose: Sugars used by yeasts during fermentation.

Mash: The process of converting grain starch into sugars with hot water.

O

Original Gravity: The measure of malted sugars in the wort. This is measured after the wort has been cooled after the boil and before pitching yeast.

P

Points per Pound per Gallon (PPG): The units of soluble extract of a malt when added to a gallon of water. It measures the change in specific gravity.

R

Racking: Transferring of beer from one container to another.

S

Sparge: Rinsing grains using hot water during the lautering process.

Steeping: The soaking of grains to soften them and extract sugars for brewing.

Strike Water: water used for a mash

Sweet Wort: Wort before the boil and before hops are added.

T

Tannins - Polyphenol compounds in grain husks or hop cones that can cause haze and bitterness in beer.

Trub – The sediment of hop bits and dead yeasts at the bottom of the kettle.

W

Wort – Unfermented beer.

Wort Chiller: A setup with copper tubes used to run water and chill the wort.

Index

adjuncts, 52, 78, 126
airlock, 34, 44
all grain brewing, 19, 20, 29, 48, 64, 76, 79, 81, 82, 88, 89, 90, 91, 93
alpha acid, 55
Aquascaping, 2, 3, 12
barley, 23, 29, 30, 48, 49, 51, 52, 115, 126
base malts, 50, 76, 78, 82, 92
Basic Brewing Steps, 22, 31
Batch sparging, 84, 92
Beer color, 26
beer machine, 13
BIAB, 89, 93
bittering hops, 54
bottle capper, 97, 99, 110
Bottle conditioning, 23
bottle wand, 102, 110
brew in a bag, 89
brewing processes, 19, 29, 30, 48, 53, 56
caramel malts, 50, 51

carbonation, 23, 102, 103, 104, 105, 106, 110, 111, 126
carboy, 34, 36, 39, 58
chiller, 42, 61, 62, 87, 93
CO_2, 95, 102, 103, 104, 105, 109, 110, 111, 125, 126
cool the wort, 86
corn, 49, 52, 95, 109, 115, 126
Cornelieus, 107, 111
Davidson guide, 27
Dimethyl Sulfide, 109, 111, 126
DMS, 109, 111, 126
Dry Dock Brewing Co, 16, 17
enzymes, 23, 48, 51
extract brewing, 20, 21, 28, 29, 30, 40, 42, 48, 58, 76, 79, 81, 86, 91, 93, 97, 110
Extract brewing, 19, 29, 30
fermentable sugars, 23, 77, 82, 84, 91, 125
fermenting, 13, 23, 39, 40, 56, 69, 76, 125, 127

fly sparging, 84, 85, 86, 92
George Washington, 16
Home Brewers Association, 15
Home brewing laws, 112, 118
hop plant, 53
hydrometer, 25, 31, 43, 45, 94, 125
IBUs, 55, 120
International Bitterness Units, 55
J.W. Lovibond, 26
kegs, 17, 72, 103, 104, 105, 107, 108, 110, 111
kilning, 49, 50
kit, 12, 13, 15, 21, 28, 29, 30, 32, 39, 40, 41, 44, 47, 48, 81, 97, 110, 117
kits, 13, 15, 32, 39, 40, 41, 45, 47, 58, 72, 80, 88, 100, 117, 126
lauter tun, 64, 83, 84
Malt Color Units, 28
malt extract, 15, 19, 20, 21, 22, 28, 30, 40, 41, 48, 56, 58, 76, 80, 81, 82, 90, 126
mashing, 20, 76, 77, 78, 79, 82, 84, 85, 87, 90, 91, 92, 109, 126, 128

Mashing, 23, 76, 82, 91, 92
MCU, 28
Noble hops, 55
oats, 49, 52, 115
partial mash brewing, 20, 29, 79, 80
Partial mash brewing, 19, 30, 76
pH, 86, 92, 93
President George Washington, 14
President Jimmy Carter, 14, 112
President Obama, 15
primary fermentation, 96
primary fermenter, 45, 87
rice, 49, 52, 115
rocks, 2, 3
rye, 49, 52, 53, 115
sanitation, 69, 71, 74
sanitize, 41, 70, 72, 73, 74, 101, 102, 110
sanitizer, 41, 72, 73, 74
secondary fermentation, 24, 45, 96, 126
secondary fermenter, 45
Specific gravity, 94
Specific Gravity, 25, 31, 94
SRM, 26, 27, 28

Standard Reference
   Method, 26
steeping, 20, 23, 24, 30, 41,
   49, 60, 76, 77, 78, 82, 91,
   92
steeping malt, 23
stuck sparge, 85
substrate, 2, 3
Thomas Jefferson, 14, 16
wheat, 26, 49, 51, 52, 115

wort, 23, 24, 28, 29, 30, 32,
   42, 54, 55, 56, 59, 61, 62,
   63, 64, 71, 73, 74, 77, 81,
   82, 83, 84, 85, 86, 87, 88,
   91, 92, 93, 109, 111, 116,
   125, 126, 127, 128, 129
yeast, 14, 15, 23, 29, 30, 32,
   39, 42, 47, 48, 53, 56, 69,
   73, 76, 86, 87, 88, 93, 94,
   95, 96, 116, 125, 127, 128

Home Brewing

www.ingramcontent.com/pod-product-compliance
Lightning Source LLC
LaVergne TN
LVHW051245080426
835513LV00016B/1743